ETHICS COMPANION

BERNARD ROSEN
The Ohio State University

PRENTICE HALL, *Englewood Cliffs, New Jersey 07632*

Library of Congress Cataloging-in-Publication Data

Rosen, Bernard.
    Ethics companion / Bernard Rosen.
        p.   cm.
    Includes bibliographical references.
    ISBN 0-13-291691-6
    1. Ethics--Handbooks, manuals, etc.   I. Title.
BJ1012.R57   1989
170--dc20   89-39735
                                                          CIP

To Peter Horn, a friend, and a friend of philosophy.
His love of philosophy and commitment to the highest standards of its
teaching are an inspiration to all of us.

Editorial/production supervision and
    interior design: Lisa A. Domínguez
Cover Design: Photo Plus Art
Manufacturing Buyer: Mike Woerner

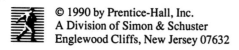

© 1990 by Prentice-Hall, Inc.
A Division of Simon & Schuster
Englewood Cliffs, New Jersey 07632

Printed in the United States of America
10 9 8 7 6 5 4 3 2 1

ISBN 0-13-291691-6

Prentice-Hall International (UK) Limited, *London*
Prentice-Hall of Australia Pty. Limited, *Sydney*
Prentice-Hall Canada Inc., *Toronto*
Prentice-Hall Hispanoamericana, S. A., *Mexico*
Prentice-Hall of India Private Limited, *New Delhi*
Prentice-Hall of Japan, Inc., *Tokyo*
Simon & Schuster Asia Pte. Ltd., *Singapore*
Editora Prentice-Hall do Brasil, Ltda., *Rio de Janeiro*

Contents

CHAPTER 3   Finalists   45

Preface

Ethics Companion is designed to be a companion to ethics anthologies for courses in theoretical, applied, or professional ethics. Anthologies contain selections by different authors in ethical theory or on particular topics such as price fixing, abortion, child abuse, or nuclear disarmament. The theoretical articles present important views by authors such as Kant or Mill, whereas the topical articles raise moral issues and typically offer solutions to them. Students are expected to evaluate the theories and arguments and compare them with positions and arguments offered in other articles. This critical evaluation and comparison requires a common framework within which these activities take place. The framework is usually supplied by the editor of the anthology in a very short section that only rarely tells students how to compare and select among competing normative ethical theories such as utilitarianism and kantianism. Most anthologies present a sketch of two or three ethical theories and some philosophical tools. The very good student may learn from these short sections but most need more help than they provide. The instructor will have to provide much of the required background, taking significant time from the discussion of the merit of theories or the specific issues to make sure students will be able profitably to read the selections. While no text can replace an instructor, for there are always issues that require clarification and topics that require further explanation, this work is intended to be a text instructors can rely on to provide most of the background and tools so they can spend more of their time on the articles in the anthologies. This is a text that can be assigned by instructors to students taking a reading course in theoretical, applied, or professional ethics. It is sufficiently detailed for the good student to understand it and to be able to apply it with a minimum of guidance from the instructor.

This work will provide an overview of a "traditional" course in ethics. In these courses students read the original works of authors such as Aristotle, Aquinas, Hume, Kant, Mill, and Moore. *Ethics Companion* will enable students to recognize and understand the central issues addressed by the various authors, a task otherwise made difficult by the absence of a common framework and vocabulary.

I would like to acknowledge the debt I owe to my students at Ohio State University. In my attempt to understand and address what troubled them philosophically I was lead to the approach in this work. I benefited from suggestions of Andrew Swift, a graduate student at Ohio State who used the work in manuscript form. I am also immensely grateful for the help Alana Shindler provided both in the preparation of the manuscript and in her support for the project.

I would like to acknowledge my debt to the reviewers for their many suggestions on how best to present the material. Those reviewers were Matthias T. Schulte, Montgomery College; Richard Conrath, Central Maine Vocational Technical Institute; and Ronald Glass, University of Wisconsin-La Crosse.

CHAPTER 1

Introduction

Everyone faces moral problems. The physician who becomes aware of a colleague who incorrectly diagnosed several patients, and yet remains silent, makes a moral decision. To say nothing while knowing a colleague is harming patients is to take some of the moral responsibility, to become a moral actor in the situation. The student who uses material from another student's paper on the grounds that it is all right to do because "everyone does it" is endorsing and using an ethical theory. The ethical theory is a form of ethical relativism, a view that will be examined in detail in this work. The nurse who waits for five minutes before calling for help for a terminally ill elderly patient who has suffered his third cardiac arrest is making a moral decision. It is better for the patient not to suffer any longer, for any time left will be of such low quality it will be of negative benefit to the patient and to the family.

Moral problems and decisions range from the very important to the everyday. The decision about whether to give the shabbily dressed person the quarter asked for is typically a moral decision. You think, perhaps, the person will only buy cheap wine or will only be encouraged to stay on the streets. Perhaps you think the person really needs the money for food. It is more important, you think, to err on the side of trusting the person because it will result in less harm. If the person buys food, that is good, for the person is hungry. If the money is used to buy wine, that is not good, but the harm is less than would occur if the money would be used for food but is not obtained. Many of us reason this way.

In this work you will learn how to make your moral reasoning more explicit. You will learn how to use an ethical theory to help you make difficult moral decisions. As a first step in understanding your own view, it will be helpful to read the options in the ethics survey that follows. The survey contains both ethical theory material and specific topics in applied and professional ethics. The views are stated in unqualified form so you can more easily recognize your own position. At the end of the term you should look again at the passages to see how your understanding has increased. Some of the passages are in a condensed form, so you may have to read them a few times to make sure you have understood the positions. After taking the course you will see how much easier it is to read the passages that gave you so much trouble at the beginning.

ETHICS SURVEY

This is a survey of your moral views as you begin the study of ethics. You are not graded on this exercise, nor is there some set of views you are supposed to choose. No one but you and your instructor will know your position. You are asked to choose the passages that *now* seem to you to be correct, both with respect to the conclusion and to the reasoning used to arrive at it. At the end of the course your instructor may ask you to evaluate your own answers, but you will then be graded on the quality of your evaluation, not on the basis of your original answers.

The survey contains pairs of passages with incompatible conclusions. You will be asked which passage contains the conclusion you are most inclined to accept now. The arguments are made as persuasive as possible, so you may sometimes be tempted by both passages. However, since the passages contain *incompatible* conclusions, you cannot choose both. You must choose the *one* passage and its conclusion that seem best by answering the questions that follow each pair of passages.

The first half of the survey contains passages about normative ethical theory, and the second half is concerned with specific moral issues.[1]

In the following passages, the conclusion derived from each set of statements is printed in **boldface.**

I. RELATIVISM

A. 1. Value judgments differ among different cultures. 2. We in the U.S. think it wrong to cast aged parents out to sea on ice floes, but the Eskimos think it is their filial duty. 3. Most Hindus and Buddhists think it is immoral to eat meat, but most Westerners think it is morally permitted. 4. The hypothesis that best explains these and many other similar anthropological facts of cultural relativity is ethical relativism. 5. So, the conclusion is that ethical relativism is correct: **The acceptabil-**

---

[1] Instructors may wish to add other passages or choose just some sample of the ones provided. I have my students indicate their choices on a separate answer sheet so I can tabulate the results and hand them out to the class. Students like to see how others have answered, and it also gives the instructor an idea of which issues need to be clarified. Any instructor who would like to see how their classes compare with mine is welcome to see my results, and if you have a copy of yours I would like to see them.

ity, that is, the correctness or truth, of moral and value judgments is relative to the predominant moral beliefs of one's culture.

B. 1. There are some unacceptable consequences of saying that moral and value judgments are relative to the predominant moral beliefs of one's culture. 2. For example, we would have to agree that the deprivation of the civil rights of the Bahai and other non-Muslims in Iran is morally permissible in that country since the vast majority of Iranians endorse that policy. 3. In addition, for the same reason we would have to agree that slavery in the U.S. in the eighteenth century was morally acceptable and that the Nazi's killing six million Jews, Gypsies, and Slavs was morally acceptable. 4. It is the relativity of moral judgments that leads to these unacceptable conclusions. 5. So, **we are justified in rejecting ethical relativism, the view that the acceptability of moral and value judgments is relative to one's culture.**

QUESTIONS

1. The conclusion I am most inclined to agree with is in passage (*circle one*): A   B.
2. In the passage containing the conclusion I did not choose, the sentence(s), *other than the conclusion,* I reject are (*write numbers*)
3. The passage containing the conclusion I am most inclined to agree with contains some sentence(s) with which I do not agree. The number(s) is (are)

II. PREFERENCE

A. 1. When someone makes a moral judgment, such as "The use of surrogate mothers is wrong," it is usually relevant to ask for reasons. 2. The reasons given include: "The practice would, if accepted, result in the weakening of the family, and it would lead to baby selling." 3. Now, of course, we may disagree with this conclusion and consequently offer our own reasoning to replace it, but we recognize the appropriateness of the procedure. 4. This procedure is the giving, evaluating, accepting, and rejecting of reasons, something that is not just a matter of preference. 5. Thus, **moral judgments are not just a matter of preference.**

B. 1. Two people can agree about all the observable, factual characteristics of vanilla and strawberry ice cream, and yet one prefers vanilla to strawberry and the other chooses strawberry over vanilla. 2. This is true of all matters of preference, of which taste is but one instance. 3. Disagreements about such matters often outlast factual agreement about the matter at hand. 4. A moral example will show how this applies to ethics: Two people will frequently agree that capital punishment does not significantly deter crime, and yet one will hold that we morally ought to have a capital punishment law and the other the opposite view. 5. This kind of phenomenon shows that **moral judgments are primarily a matter of preference.**

QUESTIONS

1. The conclusion I am most inclined to agree with is in passage (*circle one*): A   B.
2. In the passage containing the conclusion I did not choose, the sentence(s), *other than the conclusion,* I reject are (*write numbers*)

3. The passage containing the conclusion I am most inclined to agree with contains some sentence(s) with which I do not agree. The number(s) is (are)

III. ABSOLUTES

A. 1. Moral rules are stated without qualification, or they are useless. 2. For example, "lying is wrong" has to have the force of "all lying is wrong." 3. But, we know that it is sometimes not wrong to lie. 4. For example, if your mother asks if you like the special meal she made for your birthday, you are usually not doing the wrong thing in lying when you do not much care for it but tell her that you do. 5. Moral rules stated without qualification are absolutes, and absolute rules are not acceptable. 6. Morality requires such absolute rules. 7. So, **moral judgments are themselves not acceptable.**

B. 1. Moral rules contain an implicit "all things being equal" clause. 2. We should not lie, all things being equal. 3. However, when we would hurt our mother, bring about greater harm, or violate a weightier moral consideration, we are morally justified in lying. 4. We know we are sometimes morally justified in lying, and moral rules as so interpreted allow this. 5. With this understanding, then, **moral judgments are acceptable when they are so interpreted.**

QUESTIONS

1. The conclusion I am most inclined to agree with is in passage (*circle one*): A   B.
2. In the passage containing the conclusion I did not choose, the sentence(s), *other than the conclusion*, I reject are (*write numbers*)
3. The passage containing the conclusion I am most inclined to agree with contains some sentence(s) with which I do not agree. The number(s) is (are)

IV. EGOISM—MOTIVES

A. 1. When someone does something voluntarily, they do it because they want to. 2. Whatever we do for this reason is done to satisfy that want. 3. Wants, when satisfied, benefit the person whose wants they are. 4. This shows that **our only or primary motive in any voluntary action is to benefit ourselves.**

B. 1. Some, perhaps even most, of our motives in voluntary action are to benefit ourselves, but some are to benefit others. 2. When we open a door for someone whose arms are full of books or packages, a person we have never seen before and are not likely to see again, our primary motive is usually to help that person get through the door, not primarily to benefit ourselves. 3. This kind of voluntary action commonly occurs. 4. Therefore, **it is not true that our only or primary motive in any voluntary action is to benefit ourselves.**

QUESTIONS

1. The conclusion I am most inclined to agree with is in passage (*circle one*): A   B.
2. In the passage containing the conclusion I did not choose, the sentence(s), *other than the conclusion*, I reject are (*write numbers*)

3. The passage containing the conclusion I am most inclined to agree with contains some sentence(s) with which I do not agree. The number(s) is (are)

V. EGOISM—JUDGMENTS

A. 1. We make many moral and value judgments that are about future events. 2. For example, we think it right or even obligatory to set aside wilderness areas for future development of parks, to limit population so future generations will live reasonably well, and to buy life insurance. 3. We often judge that a certain course of action is right because of the benefit others will receive. 4. When we are dead, nothing that happens (on earth at least) will benefit us or hurt us. 5. This shows that **moral judgments are based not only on an assessment of our own self-benefit and self-interest.**

B. 1. Consider the hypothesis that when individuals judge that an action is right they do so on the basis of the benefit each thinks he or she will receive from that action. 2. For example, the judgment that the U.S. ought to increase (or decrease) defense spending is based on thinking that more (or less) defense spending will make me more secure. 3. Sometimes my interests and your interests coincide, and then we have a common moral position. 4. This is the nature of moral judgments: **They are based wholly on an assessment of our own self-benefit and self-interest.**

QUESTIONS

1. The conclusion I am most inclined to agree with is in passage (*circle one*): A   B.
2. In the passage containing the conclusion I did not choose, the sentence(s), *other than the conclusion*, I reject are (*write numbers*)
3. The passage containing the conclusion I am most inclined to agree with contains some sentence(s) with which I do not agree. The number(s) is (are)

VI. RIGHTS OF COUNTRIES

A. 1. Countries have the right of self-defense. 2. On occasion this right requires that some members of the country give up their life or liberty rights. 3. For example, as a soldier you may be given a lawful order that leads to your death, but in most instances you are legally and morally obligated to obey it. 4. You are not typically justified in exercising your individual freedom to disobey such an order. 5. This shows that **collectives such as countries have at least some basic rights.**

B. 1. Individuals have basic rights such as life and liberty. 2. Collectives such as countries have only those rights given to them by individuals. 3. So, **collectives such as countries have no basic rights.**

QUESTIONS

1. The conclusion I am most inclined to agree with is in passage (*circle one*): A   B.
2. In the passage containing the conclusion I did not choose, the sentence(s), *other than the conclusion*, I reject are (*write numbers*)

3. The passage containing the conclusion I am most inclined to agree with contains some sentence(s) with which I do not agree. The number(s) is (are)

VII. ULTIMATE VALUE

A. 1. We value various things, such as friendship, pleasure, love, and freedom. 2. All of these, however, will come to an end. 3. Indeed, since each of us will die, each of the things we value will come to an end. 4. If we wish to find some value to our life as a whole, we must find something that is of value forever, something whose value is eternal. 5. Therefore, **if there is not something of this sort, something of ultimate value, then none of the things we now value are valuable at all.**

B. 1. We think that pleasurable experiences are valuable and painful ones disvaluable. 2. When the pain ends it is still true that our experience was disvaluable. 3. If disvalue does not require that something be disvaluable forever, then there is no reason to think that a value such as pleasure or freedom needs to be valuable forever. 4. Furthermore, value requires contrast; we would not appreciate the value of pleasure if pleasure was all we had. 5. But, since there is a contrast, pleasurable experiences must end. 6. For these 2 reasons we can see that **there need not be anything of ultimate value for some things, for example, love or freedom, to have value.**

QUESTIONS

1. The conclusion I am most inclined to agree with is in passage (*circle one*): A   B.
2. In the passage containing the conclusion I did not choose, the sentence(s), *other than the conclusion,* I reject are (*write numbers*)
3. The passage containing the conclusion I am most inclined to agree with contains some sentence(s) with which I do not agree. The number(s) is (are)

VIII. WAR

A. 1. Present U.S. and Soviet defense policies depend on each side having the capacity to destroy the other. 2. This policy of mutual assured destruction (MAD) has prevented nuclear war for the past thirty-five years. 3. So, **we should preserve our nuclear arsenal.**

B. 1. There can be no limited nuclear war. 2. Once nuclear weapons are used, the inevitable escalation will result in the destruction of all life—with the possible exception of hardy life such as cockroaches. 3. If we disarm unilaterally, the worst thing that can happen is a long period of tyranny under Soviet rule. 4. However, we have a much stronger obligation to preserve life on earth than to fight to protect our country. 5. So, **we should now, unilaterally if necessary, destroy our nuclear arsenal.**

QUESTIONS

1. The conclusion I am most inclined to agree with is in passage (*circle one*): A   B.
2. In the passage containing the conclusion I did not choose, the sentence(s), *other than the conclusion,* I reject are (*write numbers*)

3. The passage containing the conclusion I am most inclined to agree with contains some sentence(s) with which I do not agree. The number(s) is (are)

IX. WAR IS HELL

A. 1. When fighting a war of national survival, one must use whatever means necessary to win. 2. Moral concerns, such as avoiding inflicting casualties on civilians, must not be allowed to stay our military strategy, for otherwise we might lose. 3. So, **the notion of morality does not apply in war.**

B. 1. We fight wars not just to survive but to survive as the nation that values such things as human life and freedom. 2. It would be pointless to fight a war that we win only because we give up our national moral character. 3. So, **the notion of morality does apply in war.**

QUESTIONS

1. The conclusion I am most inclined to agree with is in passage (*circle one*): A   B.
2. In the passage containing the conclusion I did not choose, the sentence(s), *other than the conclusion,* I reject are (*write numbers*)
3. The passage containing the conclusion I am most inclined to agree with contains some sentence(s) with which I do not agree. The number(s) is (are)

X. ABORTION

A. 1. A fetus is a living human being, not a lizard or wart. 2. Living human beings have a life right. 3. Life rights generate an obligation on the part of others not to kill the being who has it. 4. Abortion consists of killing a human fetus. 5. So, **there is an obligation not to perform abortions.**

B. 1. A "living human being," a being with rights, is a creature with cerebral brain activity. 2. Before the second trimester of development, until approximately the twelfth week, there is no such brain activity. 3. When there is no "live human being," there is no human with a life right. 4. The first-trimester fetus is thus seen not to be a live human being with a life right. 5. Therefore, **there is no obligation not to perform abortions within the first trimester or about twelve weeks into the pregnancy.**

QUESTIONS

1. The conclusion I am most inclined to agree with is in passage (*circle one*): A   B.
2. In the passage containing the conclusion I did not choose, the sentence(s), *other than the conclusion,* I reject are (*write numbers*)
3. The passage containing the conclusion I am most inclined to agree with contains some sentence(s) with which I do not agree. The number(s) is (are)

XI. EUTHANASIA

A. 1. In the course of some illnesses there is overwhelming evidence that the person will shortly die. 2. Miracles can happen, but we have to make decisions on the basis of what is most likely to happen, given the evidence. 3. On those occasions of imminent death, where the person is suffering greatly, where there is overwhelming evidence the person will die shortly, and the person chooses to die, a quicker death would have the effect of reducing the person's suffering. 4. We have some obligation to end suffering when requested. 5. So, **on those occasions when a terminally ill person who is suffering greatly requests a physician to end his or her life with a painless injection, the physician has an obligation to administer the injection.**

B. 1. When people are in great pain they do not think very clearly. 2. When someone is not thinking very clearly we do not take that person's requests to be binding, especially on matters of life and death. 3. On the other hand, if a patient is not in great pain, there is no reason to end life more quickly. 4. Physicians, after all, are the preservers of life and not the destroyers of life. 5. Since terminally ill patients are either in great pain or not, the conclusion is inescapable. 6. Thus, **physicians never have an obligation to end a terminally ill patient's life with a painless injection.**

QUESTIONS

1. The conclusion I am most inclined to agree with is in passage (*circle one*): A   B.
2. In the passage containing the conclusion I did not choose, the sentence(s), *other than the conclusion,* I reject are (*write numbers*)
3. The passage containing the conclusion I am most inclined to agree with contains some sentence(s) with which I do not agree. The number(s) is (are)

XII. HOMOSEXUALITY

A. 1. If someone wanted to eat a live chicken in a public park, we would not hesitate to prevent this disgusting activity. 2. Freedom of action is properly restricted when a vast majority of persons find the action disgusting. 3. The vast majority of Americans find homosexual activity disgusting. 4. For example, a homosexual dance, that is, one advertised as being for homosexuals, is something most people would find offensive, and known homosexuals teaching at the elementary school level is something that would repel most people. 5. So, **it is morally permissible to prevent such events from taking place.**

B. 1. We are justified in restricting actions of persons only when their actions are likely to harm others. 2. Homosexual activities are not likely to harm others. 3. People may be offended, but there is almost no action that does not offend someone or other. 4. Those who are offended by homosexual dances or the sight of homosexuals teaching school need not witness those events. 5. So, **it is not morally permissible to restrict such events from taking place.**

QUESTIONS

1. The conclusion I am most inclined to agree with is in passage (*circle one*): A   B.
2. In the passage containing the conclusion I did not choose, the sentence(s), *other than the conclusion,* I reject are (*write numbers*)

3. The passage containing the conclusion I am most inclined to agree with contains some sentence(s) with which I do not agree. The number(s) is (are)

XIII. RACIAL QUOTAS

A. 1. In the past, American blacks have been denied equal access to jobs and education. 2. This has resulted in fewer blacks in the more highly desirable jobs and occupations. 3. In order to rectify this past injustice we should now set a quota for blacks in such jobs. 4. That is, **we should set aside a certain percentage of places in educational programs and professions for blacks.**

B. 1. Rectification of past injustice applies to individuals but not to classes of individuals. 2. If a corporation cheats someone out of money, that company has to pay back the person whose money it has taken. 3. Quotas are not an effective way to pick out those individuals who have been discriminated against. 4. In fact, many of the blacks now being given places in medical school or positions at corporations such as IBM are children of professionals; they need no special treatment to succeed. 5. Furthermore, since everyone in the country belongs to some minority, the minimum quotas would become maximum limits. 6. This would require, for example, a limit to the percentage of blacks in the National Basketball Association, for otherwise some other group would be deprived of its share of positions. 7. This all shows, **that we should not set aside any places for blacks in educational programs or professions.**

QUESTIONS

1. The conclusion I am most inclined to agree with is in passage (*circle one*): A   B.
2. In the passage containing the conclusion I did not choose, the sentence(s), *other than the conclusion,* I reject are (*write numbers*)
3. The passage containing the conclusion I am most inclined to agree with contains some sentence(s) with which I do not agree. The number(s) is (are)

XIV. ECONOMIC DISTRIBUTION

A. 1. The distribution of material goods, things of economic value, should be through the market mechanism. 2. This means that those who want goods purchase them at the best price they can, while those who sell them get the best price they can. 3. Even though it may sound cruel, the government should not be responsible for distributing any goods to anyone. 4. Those who are unable to earn a living will have to be supported by voluntary agencies. 5. Private caring for those unable to earn a living is the only way to avoid the bad consequences of waste, encouraging dependence on the government, and weakening the economy. 6. So, **only the market mechanism should determine who acquires economic goods.**

B. 1. We have a collective obligation to those in our society who are unable to earn a living. 2. There is only one agency through which we can, realistically, discharge this obligation, namely, the government. So, **the government, on some appropriate level, should support those unable to support themselves.**

QUESTIONS

1. The conclusion I am most inclined to agree with is in passage (*circle one*): A   B.
2. In the passage containing the conclusion I did not choose, the sentence(s), *other than the conclusion*, I reject are (*write numbers*)
3. The passage containing the conclusion I am most inclined to agree with contains some sentence(s) with which I do not agree. The number(s) is (are)

ETHICS SUBJECT MATTER

MORALITY

Ethics, the study of morality by philosophers, is but one study of morality. Morality is also studied by sociologists, psychologists, theologians, politicians, economists, novelists, and poets. They frequently attend to the very same phenomena but each from the perspective of their own discipline. For example, all are interested in whether abortion should be allowed "on demand" in the first trimester. The politician might wonder whether to vote for a constitutional amendment prohibiting these abortions; a novelist could write about the anguish of a woman contemplating abortion; and a psychologist may study the effects on those who have had abortions. An economist can inform us of the cost of prohibiting abortions as measured in terms of lost income, use of institutions for unwanted children, and the economic loss from women whose education is interrupted.

Notice that I assume the reader recognizes what a moral issue is. When there is some difficulty in recognizing a moral issue, the context is usually enough to tell if we are talking about a moral 'should' or a legal 'should'. Moral judgments using 'ought' are typically easy to recognize, but people sometimes use 'ought' and other moral terms in many ways in one sentence. "If you want to get elected you ought to vote for the Equal Rights Amendment, which gives women what they ought to have anyway." Two examples of equivocal uses are "You ought to hire more women" and "You ought not to park in the fire lane." There can be a moral *and* a legal sense of 'ought' in both claims.

A helpful definition of ethics is not available, but then again, helpful definitions are not available for most subjects. One could say that physics studies physical phenomena, but we would all notice that 'physical' is a large part of the meaning of 'physics'. The best that can be done is to say that ethics is the philosophical investigation of moral phenomena. In the next chapter the reader will see by example what ethics is. In the meantime, though, here is a clear example of the kind of moral argumentation that goes on and forms part of the moral phenomena we shall study.

The dispute about abortion is typically a moral one. Let us lay out the argument mentioned so we can better evaluate it. There is no hope or aim of settling this very thorny issue; the following argument, one of the earliest on this issue, is intended only to make clear the kinds of arguments that are used. "P" in the argument stands for *premise* and "C" for *conclusion*. A premise is a statement that is supposed to support the conclusion.

```
P1. If any action is an instance of murder, then we ought
to prohibit it.
P2. Abortion is an instance of murder.
Therefore, C₁. We ought to prohibit abortion.
P3. If an action ought to be prohibited, then we ought to
pass a law forbidding its occurrence.
P4. Abortion is an action that ought to be prohibited (from
previous argument).
Therefore, C₂. We ought to pass a law forbidding abortion.
```

In the argument, we did not write 'morally ought' because the context makes it clear that we are using 'ought' in the moral sense. This is a moral argument, one that all of you have heard or read in some form or other. This argument, though, does not settle the moral issue of abortion; it signals the beginning of a clearer discussion of it. If you are using this book in a course in which this topic is addressed more fully, you will now have to discuss the question of whether P2 and P3 are true. There are many other arguments on this topic, as you will discover if you read some articles or discuss this issue in class. The laying out of the argument shows, though, the kind of clarity one can bring to issues using some of the traditional techniques of philosophy. This clarity does not, by itself, settle the moral issues, but it does allow significant progress toward this end. The clarity also allows us better to see where we begin our investigation and our attempted explanation of moral phenomena.

Moral Terms and Normative Ethical Theories

I have assumed that all of us understand the clearest moral terms such as 'right' and 'ought'. We shall not do what many non-philosophers think is most essential in doing philosophy, namely, define our basic terms. The most important kinds of definitions are those that are supported by a theory in the area. Newton did not make progress in physics by defining 'force'; its definition was a result of his physical theory. Until we have some theories before us that are reasonably well supported, no important definitions can be given. For now I shall distinguish two questions about morality and introduce a few more moral notions. The two questions are

```
(1) What do the various moral terms mean? and (2) How do we
tell when those moral terms properly apply?
```

I shall take up the first question by noting that there are three distinct moral notions that use the letters r-i-g-h-t. There is nothing wrong or distressing about this, but since we need to be clear about which sense we are using and wish to avoid confusion, we need a more precise vocabulary.

The first sense involves actions of persons: We make a positive moral evaluation of actions by saying "You performed the **right action**." "President Bush did the right thing in agreeing to reduce acid rain." Someone might disagree with this claim, perhaps substituting 'wrong' for 'right', but in each instance the moral claim would be about the action of a person. In the first instance a positive moral evaluation of the action is made ('right'), and in the second a negative moral evaluation ('wrong') is offered. If someone saves a person from drowning, we usually judge that the action is right, whereas holding the person under the water to cause drowning is wrong.

A second sense also involves actions of persons, but no positive moral evaluation is made. "Bush has a right to support aid to the Nicaraguan contras." Most people do not mean that Bush's action of saying "I am personally in favor of such aid" is a right action or one that has positive moral worth. In most instances what is meant is that the President has no moral obligation to abstain, that he is not morally forbidden from expressing his opposition. When there is an absence of an obligation to do something, we frequently use 'right to' as a description, but another term will let us say what we want without confusing our claim with the other two. This is the term **'permission'**. It is not an ordinary way of speaking, but it is comprehensible to say "Reagan is permitted to express his opposition to abortion." Permission claims are especially important when someone thinks we have an obligation to do (or not to do) something and we wish to assert our disagreement. "I am permitted to disagree with the government policy on nuclear testing—that does not make me a traitor or a disloyal citizen." Since there is the danger of confusing permission with right action and more danger in confusing it with rights, I shall henceforth use 'permission' rather than 'right to' in this work.

The third moral notion indicated by the letters r-i-g-h-t is that of **RIGHTS**. Thomas Jefferson tells us in the Declaration of Independence that we are all of us "endowed by our creator with certain inalienable RIGHTS; and that among these are life, liberty and the pursuit of happiness." When we talk about someone having a life RIGHT we do not mean that the action of living has positive moral worth, for we might think the person's living has no positive moral worth at all. For example, Hitler had a life RIGHT, though living the life he did was wrong. Saying that someone has a life RIGHT is stronger than saying that someone has a *permission* to live. If someone has a life RIGHT, then others have an obligation not to take that person's life. In contrast, if I am *permitted* to win the race, you do not thereby have an obligation to lose. We are both permitted to win; indeed, all the competitors are permitted to win. No one in the race has an obligation to lose. RIGHTS generate obligations for others, but permissions or right actions do not.

RIGHTS are usually divided into positive and negative. An easy way to draw the distinction is in terms of the kind of obligation generated by the RIGHT. A negative RIGHT is one that generates an obligation not to do something. For example, a life RIGHT is conceived as a negative RIGHT because it confers an obligation on others not to kill whoever has the life RIGHT. A health RIGHT, in contrast, is a positive RIGHT because it confers an obligation on the part of a health professional to treat. This does not establish that there are life or health RIGHTS; it only indicates how the notion of RIGHTS works by presenting common examples of negative and positive RIGHTS.

RIGHTS are true of or apply to persons, but permission and right action are true of or apply to actions of persons. It is Jefferson *the person* who has a life RIGHT, not *an action* of Jefferson. You may disagree about whether RIGHTS are inalienable or natural; you may even be skeptical about whether there are any RIGHTS at all. However, the notion of RIGHTS is different from the notions of permission and right action. To show the difference and to avoid any confusion with the other notions discussed, I use capital letters to talk about RIGHTS.

The term **'ought'** has already been used along with its opposite **'ought not'** or **'forbidden';**. We shall be somewhat informal about this and talk about 'obligation' as well. So, we can say "Males have an obligation to register with Selective Service for a possible draft" or "Males ought to register for a possible draft." Of course, we may disagree, claiming that males are permitted not to register. In all these instances, since there is a law requiring such registration, a dispute would likely be indicating the use of the moral and not the legal sense of 'ought' and its synonyms.

Some philosophers have thought that 'right' and 'ought' are redundant. All right actions, they think, are obligatory, and vice versa. However, it is now generally agreed that there are some actions that are right but not obligatory. For example, the hero who saves the rest of the patrol by throwing his body on a grenade does what is right but not obligatory. When you open the door for someone whose arms are full of books, you do something that is right since it has some small amount of positive moral worth, but it is not obligatory. This class of actions that are right but not obligatory is important enough to have its own name. They are called **supererogatory** actions.

Of the terms so far discussed, only 'RIGHTS' does not apply to the actions of persons. Another set of moral terms that applies to non-action items are **value** terms. They apply to persons, situations, experiences, institutions, things, relations, and so on. We say, for example, "Socrates was good but Hitler was bad," or "Pleasure is valuable but pain is disvaluable," or "Freedom is better than slavery," or "Love is intrinsically valuable whereas hate is intrinsically disvaluable." Value claims are not directly about the actions of persons, though, as we shall see later, they are frequently used to justify our judgments about actions. For example, consider the reasoning in: "It is wrong to hold people as slaves because slavery is evil." The value claim concerning the evil of slavery is used in a familiar way to support a judgment about the action of holding people as slaves. In this work I shall not apply value terms to actions, so as to maintain a clear distinction in the kinds of "objects" to which the two sets of terms apply. How each kind of term applies will become clearer as we examine some of the theories.

Justification and Normative Ethical Theories

The second of the two questions posed at the beginning of this section concerns the justification of moral judgments using the moral terms that have now been made somewhat clearer. It is one thing to understand what someone says with the judgment, "The U.S. ought, unilaterally if necessary, to freeze the production and deployment of nuclear weapons," and another for that judgment to be **justified** or **supported by evidence.** When we attempt to **justify** moral judgments about the actions of our country, we provide evidence of a straightforward sort; there is nothing fancy or esoteric about moral justification. A typical reason given for the claim concerning the unilateral freeze is that world peace is more likely if we carry out this action. Those who disagree will often say that world peace is endangered by a unilateral freeze. Still other persons might wonder why the issue of world peace is even relevant, and so raise the question of why world peace is thought to settle the issue. In the course of examining reasons, especially if the discussion has a structure, a point of generality will be reached that changes the nature of the enterprise. The argument in such cases employs some more general principle as seen in the following reconstruction:

```
P1. If any action increases overall good, then it ought to
be done.
P2. The action of the U.S. to freeze the production and
deployment of nuclear weapons increases overall good.
Therefore, C. The action of the U.S. to freeze the production
and deployment of nuclear weapons ought to be done.
```

In the first premise of this argument, we find a general moral claim that is a version of **utilitarianism;** the view that actions are obligatory as they tend to increase overall good. We shall examine this theory and its major variations at greater length, but for now it will serve as our model for explaining the kind of theories we shall examine. Within this form of utilitarianism, P1 of the above argument represents the highest degree of generality in justifying moral judgments about the actions of persons. The argument begins with it, and we work our way down to the judgment about the specific situation, which is usually the point in engaging in the reasoning.[2] The entire mechanism of reasoning belongs to logic as a branch of philosophy, but the first premise states the heart of a normative ethical theory.

A **normative ethical theory** or **NET** *is a device for producing specific moral judgments.* The key claim of most NETs can be captured in general statements called *principles.* Principles are used, as found above, to arrive at specific moral judgments in the conclusion. However, when we reach a conclusion using logic properly, the conclusion itself is not yet shown to be true. In addition to what we can call the formal or logical requirement, we need to have premises that are true or justified so that our conclusion is established as true as well. The following argument is formally correct (or valid), but it is not materially correct since it contains at least one false premise:

[2]In our actual reasoning we may not reach the most general point of justification until the very end of our efforts. The argument represents a reconstruction of moral reasoning; it is not a recommendation that people should reason that way. On the other hand, should you become clearer about moral reasoning, you might find this way of reasoning very clear and easy to use.

```
P1. If any creature is a snake, then it is a reptile.
P2. George Bush is a snake.
Therefore, C. George Bush is a reptile.
```

This argument is logically correct, but the conclusion is not acceptable because the second premise, P2, is not true. Note that P1 *is* true, for it does not say either that Bush is a snake or a reptile, only that *if* any creature is a snake then that creature is a reptile. And that is true even as we know he is not a snake or a reptile. So, when we reach a conclusion in the logically proper way we are not yet ready to say "Now I know that this is so, for my argument shows it." This step can only be taken when the proper evidence for the premises is also provided. If we look at the above argument about a nuclear freeze, we see that the first premise is the statement of a NET, namely, utilitarianism. It has already been pointed out that utilitarianism does not, just by itself, tell us whether we ought to have a nuclear freeze or not. We need that crucial second premise, the proposed fact about which people can disagree. But, another source of disagreement can come from a competing first premise. There are other competing NETs that would give a different conclusion. To see this, let us recast our arguments about a nuclear freeze from the viewpoint of one of utilitarianism's competitors, **ethical egoism,** and we can see a different result.

```
P1. If any action decreases my own benefit, then it ought
not to be done.
P2. The action of the U.S. to freeze the production and
deployment of nuclear weapons decreases my own good.
Therefore, C. The U.S. ought not to freeze the production
and deployment of nuclear weapons.
```

Note first of all that the negative version of egoism is used. When we replace increases with decreases, we replace the term used to indicate a positive evaluation, 'ought', with the one used to indicate a negative evaluation of an action, 'ought not'. The second thing to notice is that the second premise is startling. How could anyone say this? One reason is that the person might have evidence that if the U.S. freezes production and deployment of nuclear weapons, the likelihood of a nuclear war will increase. He or she thinks that the Soviets will then be emboldened to launch a first strike, a strike that person is not likely to live through. Or perhaps the person making the claim is a worker in a defense industry, perhaps a military officer whose career will suffer if there is a nuclear freeze. Such a person will quite likely suffer a loss of self-benefit if a freeze occurs. But, you might object, if the world is destroyed, that is not to that person's interest. To make the second premise plausible, suppose the person who presents it is about to retire and has terminal cancer that will cause death in about five years. This person might convince you that there will be no nuclear war for five years, though his evidence also shows there is then a high likelihood thereafter. At this point your disagreement would shift from the second premise to the first. That is, the disagreement would shift from one about the facts, P2, to the issue of whether the NET represented in P1, ethical egoism, is correct.

NETs with just one factor,[3] for example, the increase of my overall good, will be said to have positive and negative instances of *one* rule. For example, the following are both expressions of ethical egoism:

```
If any action increases my own good, then it is right.
If any action decreases my own good, then it is wrong.
```

The reason we need both the positive and negative versions of the rule has to do with the requirement of logically correct arguments. In the section that now follows that will be made clear.

Logic

Arguments are good or bad depending on two different considerations. One consideration has to do with the **truth of the premises** and the other with the **form of the argument.** These differences will be shown, first, for *deductive* arguments and then for *inductive* arguments. A good deductive argument, one that is **valid,** is one whose *form is such that the combination of true premises and false conclusion is not possible.* Validity is assigned to an argument in virtue of its form alone, not in virtue of the truth or falsity of its premises. The following are all valid arguments, though some have true premises (T), some false (F), some have false conclusions and some true conclusions:

```
P1. If Madonna is a father, then she is human. (T)
P2. Madonna is a father (F).
Therefore, C. Madonna is human. (T)

P1. If Madonna is a mother, then she is human. (T)
P2. Madonna is a mother. (T)
Therefore, C. Madonna is human. (T)

P1. If Madonna is a mother, then she is a reptile. (F)
P2. Madonna is a mother. (T)
Therefore, C. Madonna is a reptile. (F)

P1. If Madonna is a frog, then she is an amphibian. (T)
P2. Madonna is a frog. (F)
Therefore, C. Madonna is an amphibian. (F)
```

All of these arguments are instances of one argument form, a form called *affirming the antecedent.* The part of the "if...then..." statement following the 'if'

---

[3] A factor is a characteristic of actions. Since the factors are embedded in rules in P1, they are general. The characteristic of *increasing my overall good* will no doubt be true of many other proposed or actual actions. The egoist factor is to be contrasted with the utilitarian factor *increases the overall good.* The latter includes not just my own good but the good of all.

is called the antecedent because it comes before the second part, which is called the consequent. The argument form we shall use repeatedly in this work is a variation of affirming the antecedent sometimes called *quasi-syllogism*. An instance of this familiar form is

```
P1. If anything is human, then it is mortal.
P2. Socrates is human.
Therefore, C. Socrates is mortal.⁴
```

Each of the above arguments, regardless of the subject matter or content, is of the following valid form.

```
P1. If p, then q.
P2. p.
Therefore, C. q.
```

The above valid argument form is what all the valid arguments have in common. Indeed, they are valid because they are of this form. It is a form that does not allow the combination of (all) true premises and a false conclusion. In contrast, the following is an *invalid* argument form, so every instance of it is invalid:

```
P1. If p, then q.
P2. q.
Therefore, C. p.
```

This argument form is known as *affirming the consequent*. The following arguments are all invalid regardless of the truth or falsity of their premises:

```
P1. If Mikhail Gorbachev is a Soviet citizen, then Michael
Gorbachev is human. (T)
P2. Mikhail Gorbachev is human. (T)
Therefore, C. Mikhail Gorbachev is a Soviet citizen. (T)

P1. If Mikhail Gorbachev is a mother, then Mikhail Gorbachev
is human. (T)
P2. Mikhail Gorbachev is human. (T)
Therefore, C. Mikhail Gorbachev is a mother. (F)
```

In the second argument we have the conclusive evidence of the invalidity of the *form* called affirming the consequent. Here is an instance of an argument with

---

⁴The first premise can be *instantiated*, that is, made concrete, so it is about Socrates. Since it is about all things, it is about Socrates who is one of them.

　　If Socrates is human, then Socrates is mortal.

　　Once this legitimate logical move is made, then the argument is indeed of exactly the same form as the others presented. The move is not difficult to understand, for after all, if it is true of *anything* that if it is human, then it is mortal, then it is true of Socrates. Socrates is one of the things in the universe.

that form that has true premises and a false conclusion. That combination is not possible in a valid argument.

Another common valid argument form is *denying the consequent*, and another commonly found invalid argument form is *denying the antecedent*. The four argument forms, in an easy to see manner, can be represented as follows:

VALID	INVALID
AFFIRMING THE ANTECEDENT	AFFIRMING THE CONSEQUENT

```
P1. If p, then q.        P1. If p, then q.
P2. p.                   P2. q.
Therefore, C. q.         Therefore, C. p.
```

DENYING THE CONSEQUENT	DENYING THE ANTECEDENT

```
P1. If p, then q.        P1. If p, then q.
P2. Not q.               P2. Not p.
Therefore, C. Not p.     Therefore, C. Not q.
```

An example of denying the antecedent, the invalid argument form, that shows the invalidity of the form by the combination of true premises and false conclusion is

```
P1. If Madonna is a father, then she is human. (T)
P2. Madonna is not a father. (T)
Therefore, C. Madonna is not human. (F)
```

This combination shows clearly that the form is invalid, but even arguments of this form with true premises and true conclusions are invalid. So, the following is just as invalid as the above example:

```
P1. If Nancy Reagan is a father, then she is a male. (T)
P2. Nancy Reagan is not a father. (T)
Therefore, C. Nancy Reagan is not a male. (T)
```

When this argument is evaluated we must say the argument is invalid because it is an instance of an invalid form. If someone wishes to maintain that the conclusion is true, it must be done on the basis of something other than this argument. Of course, one would not be justified in claiming the conclusion is false because the argument is invalid. In this instance the argument is invalid and the conclusion true.

You are not expected to become a logician in order to study ethics, but this small amount of logic will help you to follow arguments more easily. Inductive arguments will be used in chapter 2 and then only in one place, so it is not necessary to say very much about inductive arguments. The contrast between inductive and deductive arguments is, though, important. A good inductive argument is *one whose premises, if true, make the conclusion probable or likely to a certain degree.* A good inductive argument, which will here be called an *acceptable argument,* can nevertheless have the combination of true premises and a false conclusion. The argument form *enumeration* will make this clear. The form is

```
P1. N% of the observed members of X are F.
Therefore, C. N% of all members of X are F.
```

This usually strikes students as a silly kind of argument, but it is very important in the social sciences when sampling techniques are used. For example:

```
P1. 80% (N) of the observed students (X) are right handed (F).
Therefore, C. 80% of all students are right handed.
```

This conclusion is likely to be true, and that likelihood increases if the sample is fair, unbiased, and adequate. However, as every pollster knows, sometimes the argument is acceptable but the conclusion is false.

This ends the preliminary material needed to make sense of what is to come. In this work you will learn how to use and evaluate various normative ethical theories or NETs. In the next chapter we shall take up theories that are significantly flawed, ones philosophers generally think are not very good ones. The examination will enable you to learn those critical skills required to evaluate NETs. This will not be simply a dry academic exercise, though, for among these theories are ones that many students are inclined to think are correct. You will recognize, no doubt, theories you have heard defended by friends or acquaintances. You yourself may be tempted by some of these theories. In learning the standard objections, you will be forced to defend your view in ways you probably have not had to use before. Thus, even if you hold the same view at the end as you did at the beginning, you will understand it better. You will certainly be able to defend it better.

In the next chapter we shall take up ethical relativism and ethical absolutism, ethical egoism, a preference theory, and a conscience view. These are theories that are thought to be so seriously flawed as NETs as to justify unqualified rejection. In the subsequent chapters the theories that have held up best in the history of thought will be examined: utilitarianism, kantianism, a prima facie (variable-weight theory), and a virtue ethics theory.

CHAPTER 2

Preliminary Theories

In the marketplace of ideas some normative ethical theories or NETs have apparently lost out. Philosophy is a very old discipline, so we have more than 2,500 years of continuous critical work to rely on. The theories in this chapter were once thought to be in the running, but as a result of past criticisms, they are no longer thought to be serious contenders for the best NET. They are still worth looking at, though, for some few philosophers and many more students still think these views are viable. An examination of many of them will be of interest to those who are inclined to hold such theories. If they wish to continue to hold those theories, however, they must be able to respond satisfactorily to the criticisms. Even if the theories are not viable, we can learn by examining them how critically to evaluate theories and how to avoid certain mistakes in the defense of our own view.

RELATIVISM AND ABSOLUTISM

Perhaps the most common criticism of a particular NET is that it supposes or uses absolutes. Since, the argument continues, there are no absolutes, that theory is mistaken. The argument concludes that the "opposite" of absolutism, relativism, is correct. In what follows I shall agree with the negative part of this critique—that there are no absolutes—but show that relativism does not follow from this conclusion.[1] I shall then show that relativism is so badly flawed that unless all the other theories are even worse we should reject it. The first step, though, is to say what absolutism is and why it is, itself, unacceptable. Since ethical absolutism and relativism are the first NETs to be examined, I shall introduce here many techniques for the examination of the other NETs. This will make for sections longer than others not because absolutism and relativism are more important but because they are the first to be examined. Relativism is picked as the first NET to examine because past surveys show that about 40% of the students hold this view.

ABSOLUTISM

I base my reconstruction of what absolutism is on many years of talking with students and others who want to reject absolutism. My study shows that an absolutist NET is one that uses *specific-factor fixed-weight rules*. What are specific factor fixed-weight rules, and why do people think there are no such things?

A **factor** is a characteristic of actions. For example, an action can be characterized as truthful or lying. Truth telling or lying are factors of some actions. When someone asks why we think that an action is right or wrong, we almost invariably describe a factor. "What makes you think what Jimmy did was wrong?" "He lied to his mother about taking the cookies." "I think what Jimmy did was right because he displayed generosity in giving a cookie to his friend Tommy." The activity of presenting factors as reasons for specific moral judgments is common and not the complaint about absolutes.

The concern about absolutes comes from supposing that the factors used in our moral rules are both of fixed weight and **specific.** In our preliminary look at utilitarianism, the factor *increases overall good* was used. This factor does not pick out a specific characteristic of an action in the same way as *lying* and *truth telling* do, so it is a **general** factor. We may disagree about what things are good and yet agree that a certain action increases overall good. General factors (for example, *overall good*) are used by theories such as egoism and utilitarianism and are in sharp contrast to the specific factors (for example, *lying* and *truth telling*) used by absolutism. To see the contrast, consider the following argument containing a rule using a specific factor:

```
P1. If any action is one of lying, then it is wrong.
P2. Jimmy's lying to his mother about taking a cookie is an
instance of lying.
Therefore, C. Jimmy's lying to his mother about taking a
cookie is wrong.
```

Is *lying* a specific-factor fixed-weight rule in this argument? There is no way to tell just by the occurrence of the term 'lying' whether it is used as a fixed-weight factor or not. However, it is definitely a fixed-weight factor if it cannot be overridden by

---

[1]This same kind of argument is still being used in contemporary philosophy. See, for example, David B. Wong, *Moral Relativity* (Berkeley: University of California Press, 1984).

other factors. One factor overrides another when its presence may change a judgment we would otherwise make about a situation. To use an earlier case, when your mother asks if you like the meal she fixed for your birthday, the factor *not hurting her feelings* overrides the factor *lying*. If lying were a fixed-weight factor, though, no matter what other factor applied, you would still be doing the wrong thing if you lied.[2]

Variable-weight factors, in contrast to fixed-weight factors, are those whose weight varies from context to context. In the context of responding to your mother's question, the weight of not hurting someone's feelings outweighs the weight of lying. In the context of telling a student whether a course was passed or not, in contrast, it goes the other way.[3] Even though the student's feelings would be hurt, it would be wrong to say "You passed the course," when that is not true. Those who hold to absolutes are those who maintain there are specific-factor fixed-weight moral rules.

What are those rules? Any rule can be taken as an absolute. Someone might hold the Ten Commandments, for example, as a NET consisting of ten absolute rules. The kind of situation sketched above, about circumstances in which the rules conflict or are clearly overridden by another, would hold of any list of proposed absolute rules. You have an absolute obligation to obey your parents and also to honor the Sabbath. What do you do when your parents command you to do something that prevents you from honoring the Sabbath? There is no problem if the rules are taken as variable in weight, but there is no solution if they are taken as absolutes. Absolutism in its various forms, consisting of sets of absolute rules, seems unworkable. Surely, then, if this view is not acceptable, as the very brief examination seems to show, and relativism is the alternative, then, the argument concludes, relativism is correct.

There are, however, a number of problems with the argument that relativism is the correct alternative. The first problem is to determine what relativism is as a NET. Let us overcome this first problem with a specification and an example of its use at the same time.

ETHICAL RELATIVISM

> P1. If any action is accepted by the majority in a culture A as being right, then it is right (in A).[4]

---

[2]We shall see, though, that the situation is a bit more complicated than this. I am here supposing that each of the fixed factors is an absolute. One could hold that there is a hierarchy of fixed-weight factors, and then the one at the top of the hierarchy would be an absolute. The others would be overridden by any of the factors higher in the hierarchy. More on this kind of view shortly.

[3]This variable-weight view will be examined more fully in the next chapter.

[4]Recall that there is a negative version of this moral principle, one that is needed in order to get out negative judgments using notions such as wrong.

> P1. If any action is accepted by the majority in a culture B as being wrong, then it is wrong (in B).
> P2. The action of hurting one's mother by telling her the special birthday meal she fixed was lousy is accepted by the majority of Americans as being wrong.
> Therefore, C. The action of hurting one's mother by telling her the special meal she fixed for your birthday was lousy is wrong.

The negative and the positive versions of the rule will be counted as one rule. The rule is counted as one because the factor used is the same one, namely, *accepted by the majority in a culture as being right or wrong.*

P2. The action of lying to one's mother when asked how one's
special birthday meal was is accepted as being right by the
majority of those in A.

Therefore, C. The action of lying to one's mother when asked
how one's special birthday meal was is right (in A).

The first premise of this argument is the principle of the NET known as ethical relativism. This NET is often defended by the following kind of argument:

P1. Either absolutism or ethical relativism is correct.
P2. Absolutism is not correct.

Therefore, C. Ethical relativism is correct.

Once again we start with a logically valid argument, so we do not have to worry about the formal conditions of its acceptability. If we can also establish that both premises are correct, we would have truly established ethical relativism. Since P2 has already been supported, that leaves only P1 to establish. Here, though, we have serious problems. In our preliminary discussion of what NETs are, we introduced utilitarianism. In addition, in setting out ethical relativism, we described yet another NET, the variable-weight view of moral factors. This means that P1 is not true, for it says that there are only two alternative competing NETs when there are at least four (absolutism, relativism, utilitarianism, and egoism).

What is the logic of this criticism? P1 is in the form of a disjunction: Either this is true or that is true. For example, "Either a number is odd or it is even." This claim is true of any whole natural number. However, when there is a third (or many additional) alternatives, then in at least one clear sense of 'or' the premise is false. As an example of this, though the subject matter is deliberately chosen so as to be as different as possible, is as follows: "Either the plane figure is a triangle or it is a circle." We might very well establish that the figure is not a triangle and yet not be justified in concluding that it is a circle. The figure may be a square, a pentagon, a hexagon, or some other figure. Unless it is true that there are only the two choices, we cannot legitimately reach the conclusion that the figure is a circle from the following premises:

P1. Either the plane figure is a triangle or it is a circle.
P2. The plane figure is not a triangle.

Therefore, C. The plane figure is a circle.

The conclusion cannot legitimately be asserted because the first premise is false since there are other alternatives.[5] The first premise of this argument is not false because we are saying that morality is like plane geometry; the premise is false because

---

[5]The argument is valid, but it is not sound because at least one of the premises is not true. The conclusion follows as a matter of logic, but because of the requirement of true premises, we are not permitted to conclude that the claim in the conclusion is true.

it shares a logical feature with a clearly false statement that happens to be about plane geometry. We could use any number of other subject matters to make the same point. For example, "The object is either red or green," "The person is either an American or a Russian," and "The celestial body is either a planet or a star." So, the first argument for the second of the NETs we have examined fails: We cannot say that relativism is correct if the argument for it rests on a false premise.

The failure of the first argument in favor of ethical relativism does not yet justify us in claiming that this NET is unacceptable, for there may be other arguments to support it. Furthermore, even if there are no positive arguments to support ethical relativism as a NET, the same may be true of all the other theories such as utilitarianism and the variable-weight theory. We would then have to determine which of these NETs did the best job in accounting for the phenomena of morality. The notion of doing the best job in accounting for the phenomena of morality is a difficult subject, but a few words here are in order. The arguments presented in the ethics survey do not begin with undeniable axioms, facts that all human beings must accept. The arguments begin with observations that most of us are inclined to accept. Those who think ethical relativism is the best NET also begin with observations we are inclined to accept. Moral judgments about specific matters such as vegetarianism and sexual preference do seem to vary among cultures. The action of saving someone from drowning does seem to be right. A NET that said that none of these *phenomena*,[6] as we shall call them, are so, that *all* of them are illusory, would have to present strong evidence to support this claim. Failing to provide this evidence, we would be justified in rejecting the NET that made the claim. Ethical relativism, as one of the NETs that attempts to explain the moral phenomena, has to be compared with others that make the same attempt. Since relativism is the first theory to be examined extensively, we can hardly compare the job it does with others, but we shall make a few preliminary comparisons now and more detailed ones later.

One more argument in favor of ethical relativism deserves examination because it too is frequently used. This is the argument found in the ethics survey, item 1A on p.2-3. This argument introduces another position known as **cultural relativism** and uses it in the attempt to establish ethical relativism. So, let us draw the distinction and then see how the argument in that passage actually goes. The view of cultural relativism usually consists of two separate claims: Moral judgments differ from culture to culture, and people adopt their moral views as the result of being educated in a certain culture. If one is raised in India the chances of coming to think that vegetarianism is the morally proper diet are much greater than if one is raised in the U.S. Cultural relativism is a claim based on observations by anthropologists and other social scientists as well as by ordinary people who visit foreign countries or observe subcultures within their own country. Since cultural relativism

---

[6] A phenomenon is something that seems to be correct as we begin any investigation; it is a starting point. A starting point of astronomy was that the sun and all the heavenly bodies moved around the earth. After several centuries of astronomical theorizing and observation to confirm or disconfirm those theories, we now say that the earth moves around the sun. So, when I say that we begin with moral phenomena, this is not to say that all the phenomena are truths. I am sure they are not, not anymore than they are truths in any other area.

is based on what is observed, it is called an **empirical theory**. It is either true or false depending on what we observe. In this instance the view seems clearly to be supported by either informal observations of travellers or the more careful observations of trained field investigators. For the purposes of the following argument we shall suppose that cultural relativism is correct. We shall not suppose, of course, that ethical relativism is correct, for that is the issue before us. To suppose that ethical relativism is correct would be to assume what has to be shown to be correct by some evidence or argumentation. If we assumed the view was correct when it is what has to be shown, that would be **begging the question.**[7] In the following argument, so we can more clearly see the structure, CR will stand for cultural relativism and ER will stand for ethical relativism.

```
P1. If CR, then ER.
P2. CR.
Therefore, C. ER.
```

This is a valid argument, being an instance of *modus ponens* or affirming the antecedent. We need to know, though, if both premises are true. It is easy to construct a logically correct argument of this form that nevertheless has one or more false premises. A clear example of such a logically correct but materially incorrect argument is as follows:

```
P1. If Ted Kennedy is a finch, then Ted Kennedy is a bird.
P2. Ted Kennedy is a finch.
Therefore, C. Ted Kennedy is a bird.
```

The form of the argument is the same as the one concerning relativism, though the subject matter is different. Let us now return to the argument on cultural and ethical relativism above. In that argument the second premise has been granted to be true, so that leaves only the first premise to examine. The first premise proposes a connection between CR and ER, but it does not tell us what it is. There are two broad categories of connection, *deductive* and *inductive,* so let us ask of each of them if it describes the connection that holds between ER and CR.

It is easy enough to show that the connection between CR and ER is not deductive by showing that the form has clear instances that go from true premises to a false conclusion. That is, the argument proposes a kind of connection that does not hold generally, for we are not permitted generally to move from a claim about disagreement to a claim about the relativity of the truth of that kind of judgment. To see this we shall have to examine other instances of doing this. The effectiveness of the examination and any conclusion we draw does not depend on comparing the subject matters but only on comparing the form or logical structure of the arguments. Keeping that in mind, consider the following:

[7]Begging the question is one mistake all philosophers agree is truly a mistake. In defending any position, everyone must take care not to make this mistake. One cannot legitimately assume what has to be shown or argued to be true.

```
P1. If people in the seventeenth century accepted that
infectious disease was caused by bad night air and imbalances
of bile, while we in the twentieth century accept that
infectious disease is caused by microorganisms, then
infectious disease was caused by bad night air in the
seventeenth century and is caused by microorganisms in the
twentieth century.
P2. People in the seventeenth century accepted that
infectious disease was caused by bad night air and imbalances
of bile, while we in the twentieth century accept that
infectious disease is caused by microorganisms.
Therefore, C. Infectious disease was caused by bad night
air and imbalances of bile in the seventeenth century and
by microorganisms in the twentieth century.
```

As usual, we have a valid argument and here a true second premise. Accordingly, it must then be the first premise that is false, for the conclusion is clearly false. But the first premise has just the connection in the first premise as is found between CR and ER. Since the logic of the two kinds of cases is the same, we must say that the connection between CR and ER is not a valid deduction. It is not a valid deduction because here is a set of claims that shares the formal characteristics and is an invalid argument. When we abstract the form of that argument, we have the following:

```
P1. People in culture B1 accept a claim p, and people in
culture B2 accept a claim not-p.
Therefore, p is true in B1, and not-p is true in B2.
```

This is not a valid deductive argument, as the above counter-example shows. So, the first premise, "If CR, then ER," if it were taken as an argument instead of a conditional statement, cannot represent a valid deductive argument since it would be of the form:

```
P1. CR.
Therefore, C. ER.
```

This form is not logically acceptable. The form is very simple.

```
P1. p.
Therefore, C. q.
```

This form is not acceptable, for anyone can make up instances that have a true premise and a false conclusion. Its unacceptability is not based on the assertion that morality is like medicine in some way or other. It is unacceptable because it has the formal characteristic of being an invalid argument.

Nevertheless, the argument that goes from CR to ER may yet be a good inductive argument. Among the many kinds of inductive arguments, the argument from CR to

ER, I suggest, is best interpreted as a **hypothetico-deductive,** or H-D, argument. This kind of argument, also called scientific method, is one that we frequently use. We pose a theory or hypothesis and then see if the predicted consequences actually follow. If they do, we conclude that the hypothesis is confirmed.

For example, we now think that infectious diseases are the result of microorganisms. In the past, people thought that disease was the result of bad air, usually the night air—or the result of being inhabited by evil spirits. A simplified discussion of this is revealed in the following argument, with h = germ theory of disease; O1 = when we examine the blood and lungs of those who have an infectious disease (such as tuberculosis) we find a microorganism (in the case of tuberculosis, the *myocobacterium tuberculosis*); O2 = the observation that when this microorganism is injected into animals who can contract the disease, and they do contract it; O3 = those who have never been exposed to the disease do not have the microorganism; h' = infectious disease is caused either by bad night air or by evil spirits.

```
P1. If h, then O1, O2, O3.
P2. O1, O2, O3.
P3. h does a better job in explaining the disease phenomena
than h'.
P4. h fits in with other related h's that are themselves
confirmed.
Therefore, C. h.
```

These premises are ones we have great confidence in because the battle between the germ theory and its major rivals is one that is over.[8] The requirement of P3 that a hypothesis has to do a better job than its existing rivals is always important. In my view, it is the key to what makes an acceptable hypothesis. The germ theory accounts for such phenomena as transmission of disease and gives a theoretical foundation for vaccination. A discussion in class of why the germ theory is the best one would be worth while and would help to fix the form of this extremely important inductive argument in mind.

Another comparison is in order. One hypothesis to explain human reproduction is that sperm contain a complete human being, a homunculus, and that the egg contains the nutrient for the growth of this homunculus. The hypothesis we think is correct is that half the newborn's genetic material is supplied by the sperm and half by the egg; there is no homunculus. While both of these hypotheses explain most of the phenomena concerning human reproduction, the contemporary genetic account is better: It explains heredity as well as the fact of reproduction, it fits in with other biological findings, it allows us to develop crops and animals suitable for certain environments. This is generally true of competing hypotheses: We choose the one that does a *better*

---

[8]This bold statement is made even though there are those, e.g., Christian Scientists, who think that disease is a result of not being in the proper relation to the divine being. There are always people who disagree with positions, almost no matter what they are. This fact of disagreement does not show that we are not justified in asserting, with great confidence, that we are correct. On the other hand, we must be prepared to look at new evidence and admit, however unlikely we now think this is, that we were mistaken.

job in explaining the phenomena, not the one that simply does *a* job in explaining the phenomena. Correct theories do not come labeled "correct"; we make a judgment based on a preponderance of evidence and on ability of theories to explain, predict, and facilitate application to problems in the world. The reader might now try to set up the two rival hypotheses in the fashion indicated above for the competing explanations of infectious disease in the H-D form.

Ethical theories, NETs, are themselves hypotheses. They are not scientific hypotheses, but they too have a range of phenomena they explain; they are directed to the quite practical end of guiding our moral choices and thus our moral life. As hypotheses, we do not choose the one that explains the moral phenomena; we choose the one that does the *best job* in explaining the moral phenomena. One phenomenon that ethical relativism nicely explains is the cultural variability of moral judgments. However, other NETs can explain that same phenomenon at least as well. Utilitarianism, for example, can explain that when the choice is between the survival of the old and the survival of the young, overall good is increased by choosing the survival of the young. In that way the entire group is more likely to survive. In the U.S. the survival of the young is not tied to the death of the elderly because we have food enough for everyone. So, on the utilitarian account the variable is what results in the overall good, not morality. In utilitarianism, morality is not relative to one's culture, though what increases overall good varies from location to location depending on available resources. The reader might try to set up the rivals of ethical relativism and utilitarianism in the hypothetico-deductive form.

Other NETs can also explain the phenomenon of cultural diversity of morals, but it is enough to show that since at least one other theory accounts for cultural diversity, ethical relativism's explanation of this phenomenon does not justify us in accepting it as the best NET. If, as it increasingly appears, ethical relativism is not viable, we must continue our search for the best NET. These criticisms are probably "enough," but since ethical relativism is so entrenched, another criticism will be presented before we go on.

The additional criticism of ethical relativism is different enough to warrant presenting it. It is the **New Problem problem.** This argument is in the form of an indirect proof, an argument form used extensively in logic and geometry. In this kind of argument one assumes the negation of what is to be argued for. The next step is to derive some absurd consequence, typically a contradiction, to show that the assumption leads to an obviously false claim. Since the assumption leads to what is not acceptable, we conclude that the assumption is false. Since the negation of the assumption is what we set out to establish, we are then in a position to assert its truth. In this instance we shall assume that ethical relativism is correct. The argument will be laid out with the steps separated so that it will be easier to follow.

```
P1. Ethical relativism (ER) is correct. (ASSUMPTION)
P2. Given that we know P1 is correct, no one can rationally
offer a justified moral judgment without using ER.
P3. There are new moral problems (one will be described
below).
```

P4. To arrive at a judgment concerning the new problem, we must use ER (P1 and P2).

P5. To use ER, we must find out what the majority believes about the moral problem (this is how ER works).

P6. In order for us to find out what the majority believes about the moral problem, individual persons must give their answer to new moral problems.

P7. For an individual rationally to answer our question about the new moral problem, that person must use ER (P4).

P8. For an individual to use ER, there must be a majority opinion about the new problem.

P9. But there is no majority opinion about the new problem (because it is a new problem).

P10. Therefore, no individual can use ER to arrive at a moral judgment about a new moral problem.

Therefore, C1. No one can arrive at a justified moral judgment about a new moral problem.

C1 is, though, a clearly false claim. The premise that leads to this clearly false claim is P1. So we are justified in rejecting that premise. That is:

Therefore, C2. Not-P1 (ER is not correct).

What kind of thing is a new moral problem? First, of course, it *is* a moral problem. We wonder whether an action is right or wrong or whether we ought to do something or not. What is a new problem depends on your temporal and spatial location. If you lived in the U.S. in the middle of the nineteenth century, slavery would have been a moral problem. Given that the constitution recognized slavery, that the Dred Scott decision upheld this interpretation, and that you have an obligation to obey the law, the reporting of runaway slaves would seem to be morally required. On the other hand, supposing slavery is morally wrong, you have an obligation or at least are permitted to help the slave to escape. This is an example of a moral problem. While all problems have *something* in common with other problems—otherwise we would not recognize them as problems—there are problems sufficiently different from ones that have occurred to call them new problems. For example, in the history of the human race the use of weapons has always posed moral problems. The desire to beat swords into plowshares is as old as recorded literature. Older yet is the knowledge that if all do not do away with their swords, those who do will be at the mercy of those who do not. Today, though, there is a new problem concerning weapons. If we use nuclear weapons in an all-out war between, say, the U.S. and the Soviet Union, the destruction of the biosphere will likely be the result, and all life will probably disappear from the earth. This is an example of a new problem.

What new problem do I want to draw your attention to so that you clearly recognize new moral problems? Any problem that I mention here will not be new by the time you read it. So, you should use your own example, or have your instructor draw one up for you. As I write this in 1989, a number of issues are before the public. What are the RIGHTS of a surrogate mother concerning the baby she contracted to deliver to those who paid her for "renting her womb"? Should AIDS be declared a handicapped condition? Should health professionals be permitted not to treat people with AIDS? Should physicians use experimental treatment on AIDS sufferers? In 1986 a team of surgeons used a non-approved artificial heart to keep a patient alive until a donor heart was found. The physicians have some obligation to save their patient, but they and the FDA also have some obligation to protect the public by not using devices of this sort until they have been tested.

These are all new problems about which there has not been time for the public to form an opinion. If you ask me or anyone what I or they think about using experimental drugs on AIDS patients or nonapproved artificial hearts, on the supposition that ER is correct, we would have to ask you what the majority believes. Not being fools and knowing that the only way to arrive at a justified moral judgment is to use the (assumed) one true view, namely ER, we need to know what the majority believes in order to use ER. But, since this is a new problem, there is no majority as yet. You are asking what we think of this case in an attempt to establish what *is* the majority view. Since there is no majority on these issues as yet we cannot answer. Every person who is asked is in the same position. No one can answer until we know what the majority view is, but no majority can exist until people answer. So, no decision can be reached on a new problem under the assumption that ER is correct. But, this is absurd, for we can obviously make rational decisions about new moral problems. Since it is the assumption of ethical relativism that leads to this absurd conclusion, ethical relativism is not correct.

There are two desperate moves that might be made. One is to deny that there are any new moral problems. This is, though, an apparent empirical falsehood. We do find moral problems sufficiently unlike ones that have occurred in the past to call them new. Furthermore, there must have been a first occurrence of each of the kinds that are now claimed to cover all cases. The New Problem would simply apply to them. A second move is to say that we can use some means other than ER to arrive at our judgments, then once we have a majority we use ER. But any answer that someone gave us would, by hypothesis, be unjustified. Suppose someone used utilitarianism or looked at the entrails of chickens and then said, "The action of using the unapproved artificial heart or drug is permitted." We would know that this was unjustified and, perhaps, irrational because the (assumed) correct NET was not used. The response, though, would have us believe that even though the original majority opinion is, by hypothesis unjustified or irrational, once we have this irrational majority, then thereafter that is the rational, justified position. This itself is not a defensible position.

ER is not a very good NET, or so the evidence so far suggests. Nevertheless, the reader will find in this section many of the basic tools that will be needed throughout this work. It might help to fix them in mind before you continue.

PREFERENCE THEORY

The theory that says, as one finds it in the ethics survey item II, that moral judgments are primarily a matter of preference is often heard defended by students. That theory, as put into our usual form, would look like this:

```
P1. If any action x is preferred over any alternative action
y by a person A, then x is right.⁹
P2. Lying about how the meal tastes is preferred by A over
the alternative of telling the truth by A.
Therefore, C. A lying about how the meal tastes is right.
```

This view seems initially plausible, for we do have a preference for the actions we think are right and an aversion to those we think are wrong. This is a phenomenon the preference theory does explain. There are, however, very serious problems with this theory that make it a very weak candidate for best NET. When we have two people who disagree about a proposed action, one preferring it and the other having an aversion to it, the action would be both right and wrong. Since the notions of *right* and *wrong* are contraries, they cannot both be true of an action at the same time. In the above example, suppose A's sibling, B, prefers telling the truth over lying. If we have accepted the preference theory this would lead to another conclusion: "Lying about how the meal tastes is wrong." Since the theory leads to the unacceptable result of contrary judgments being true we must then reject it. If any theory leads to the result that contrary statements are true at the same time, it must be rejected.[10]

One response to this criticism is to say that *it is true for B* that lying is wrong, whereas *it is true for A* that lying is right. The notion of true *for*, however, seems to

---

[9]The negative version of this view would be

    P1. If any action x is disliked more than any alternative action y by a person A, then x is wrong.

    P2. Telling the truth about how the meal tastes is disliked by A over the alternative of lying.

    Therefore, C. Telling the truth about how the meal tastes is wrong.

[10]There are those who claim that moral judgments are neither true nor false, and so to them contrary judgments are not both true at the same time. People who hold this view suppose that although moral judgments look like other claims that are true or false such as "The earth is the third planet of the solar system," they are not. Such philosophers hold that moral judgments are a kind of "pseudo-judgment," ones that have no meaning that has reference to the world.

Some who hold this view are inclined to think that meaning is reference. The meaning of 'Fido' is the dog whose name it is. This view of meaning, however, is generally agreed by philosophers to be flawed.

Another reason for supposing that moral judgments have no literal meaning is that some philosophers think that this view commits them to accepting some *object* that is the meaning of moral terms. They say there is no such thing—literally, a *thing*—as rightness, and so moral terms have no literal meaning. However, again, once we give up a referential theory of meaning, we are not tempted by this argument. Moral judgments have a function in our daily lives, and this function is the meaning. We are helped in deciding what to do, what to pursue, who to help, when to act. This is meaning enough to account for our use of terms such as 'true' and 'justified' as applied to moral claims.

The most serious position of this type is held by those who think that moral judgments are not true or false in the same sense that judgments about the planets or disease are true or false. This view will be examined in chapter 5.

be the same as the notion of belief. To say that some claim *p* is true for A is to say that A believes or accepts p. Belief or acceptance of some claim is not the same thing as that claim being justified or true. Some people think that disease is caused by evil spirits, but that view is not justified. Many people suppose that the U.S. is larger than the USSR, but belief does not make it true. We were looking for the best NET, a theory that would result in *justified* specific moral judgments. If we interpret a preference theory as arriving only at what people believe, then it does not even do the basic job of a NET. So, this attempt to save a preference theory takes it out of the running as best NET by eliminating it as a NET entirely.

There is a difference between the phrases 'true of' and 'true for'. While the latter is another way of talking about belief, the former is a way of indicating a subject or object of discourse. "It is true of Lincoln that he had a beard but not true of Kennedy." The claim "Lincoln had a beard" is true in the usual sense of true. If someone says that no U.S. President wore a beard, we can reply that Lincoln did—it is true of him.

Another reason to reject a preference theory is that it does not allow any place for reasons in making moral judgments. This is the position laid out in the ethics survey, item 11 A, a position that provides another reason to reject a preference NET. If a preference theory is correct, then reasons would not be relevant for moral judgments. But, one thing clear about moral judgments is that the giving and evaluating of reasons is a constant feature. Since a preference NET cannot adequately account for this phenomenon, that weakens the theory. An important moral phenomenon, of course, is that people have strong feelings about moral matters. When people firebomb clinics at which abortions are performed, they act on their moral judgment that abortion is murder. Important moral judgments are usually not cool appraisals; they are frequently passionate pleas that lead to passionate action. Any NET we accept should take this phenomenon into account, but it looks as though it will have to be a theory other than a preference theory.

INDIVIDUAL RELATIVISM

A NET people sometimes have in mind when they choose a preference NET is a form of relativism called **individual relativism.** This view would have as its main rule the following:

```
If any action x is believed by person A to be right, then
x is right.
```

In contrast to ethical relativism, which is a social view, this is a view about the beliefs of individual persons. Actions that are believed right are right, those believed wrong are wrong. This NET has many of the defects of ethical relativism. It cannot, for example, account for rational decisions concerning new moral problems and for changes of mind. When we have disagreements, one person believes an action is right and another denies it, and we seem to have contradictory judgments that are both true at the same time. Individual relativism also has some of the defects of a preference theory. It cannot, for example, account for the requirement that reasons to support our moral judgments. Such a theory is not worth looking at in detail, but this brief account should allow those who wish to understand such a view to see what it is and why it is not acceptable.

RELIGION AND MORALITY

In our society a good deal of moral instruction is given as part of religious instruction. Most children are taught to be kind to others and other morally proper forms of behavior in a house of worship. Moral training at home tends also to be presented within a religious context. Religious beliefs form an important and significant part of the moral stances that many, if not most, people take. When people have difficulty arriving at a moral judgment, they find it useful to think what God would do. I shall not question any of these claims. But because of such claims, there is a tendency to think that morality is dependent upon the words of God and that this is a NET that is properly used.

Another perspective sometimes leads to this same conclusion. The majority of people in the U.S. think that God made or designed the universe, including all its laws. They further think that moral laws, while different than physical laws, are just another kind of law. Finally, people think that God or some other divine being makes actions right or wrong by a decision, so we find out what is right or wrong by finding out what God judges. In this section this set of views will be examined. It will not be questioned whether God exists or not, or whether people take moral comfort and derive moral benefit from their religious beliefs. The examination that follows is solely about a quite specific NET that will be explained shortly.

MORAL KNOWLEDGE AND GOD

Scarcely a month goes by without a grisly killing in our country in which the killer claims that God told him to do it. Of course, few, if any, suppose God told the killer to do what he did. A man will kill all the children in his household, saying God told him they were possessed by the Devil, and so he should kill them all. We are saddened and horrified by these stories, and the horror is magnified by the reference to a being who is all good. But why is this?

In the Judeo-Christian-Islamic tradition, God is the all-good being who is also all knowing and all powerful. To be all powerful is to have the power to do all those things that can be described as actions. So, the building of a round square or constructing a proof that $1 + 1 = 3$ are not actions to be done at all. There is no possible figure that is a round square and no possible proof of what is a contradiction. God can do all that can be done but not what is not something to be done. To be all powerful is not to be able to do what cannot be done; it is to be able to do all that can be done. Similarly, to be all knowing is to know everything that can be known. God cannot know that $1 + 1 = 3$ because that is not true. To say that God is all good is to say that He brings about good or a balance of good over evil wherever that can be done. God's nature is good, so to say that bringing about something evil is possible for God would be to say that God is sometimes not God. God is a being whose actions are always consistent with His nature.

This is the *concept* of God, but having the concept is not the same as the being so conceived existing. Nothing in the following discussion will presume that the question of whether this being exists or not has been settled. It will be assumed, for the purpose of this discussion, that such a being exists. For those who are not believers, you will find this discussion of interest because there are so many who do believe in such a being. For those who are believers, of course, you will find this of interest because it is about a being you suppose exists.

Let us ask about our reaction to the mass murderer again. We do not think "Well, it had to be done, and it was obviously the right thing to do because, after all, God told him to do it." We do not think this because we have good reason to suppose that God did not tell the man to kill all his children. We reason, it seems to me, in the following way: "The action of killing all his children is clearly a wrong action. The children were just children, not creatures of the Devil, so what the man did is wrong. (Most of us would also suppose the killer is probably severely disturbed, so he may not be totally morally responsible for his wrong action.) Since the action is wrong, God did not tell the man to do it, for God does not tell us to do things that are wrong." This is a common way of explaining such events.

The reasoning that concludes that it was not God who told the man to kill his children allows another conclusion to be drawn. Notice that it was a *moral* test we used to decide that it was not God who told the man to kill all his children. Since we used a moral test to determine whether or not it was God who spoke to the man, we cannot say that all our moral knowledge depends upon what God says. We may look in the Bible for guidance, but even there we interpret some things and reject other things as divinely inspired on the grounds that the content is morally unacceptable and thus not from God. There is no question that many think of God as the best possible moral judge. God, being all good and all knowing, will invariably arrive at the correct moral judgment. In spite of this, we still cannot say that all or some of our basic knowledge of what is right and wrong must come from what God tells us, because we sometimes do not accept that a piece of advice has come from God because we know that the action recommended is wrong. To reject such advice, we must have moral knowledge independently of what God says. This is not to deny that God is all good, or that God created the universe and everything in it. We suppose, to take a parallel case, that God created the physical world with just the laws it has. We do not suppose, though, that we need to study religion in order to discover the laws of physics.

We suppose that some of the Biblical description of the world, for example, that it has four corners and that the earth is the center of the solar system, is not meant to be taken as literally true because it is contrary to what we know about the physical world by other means. This does not detract from God's power, so neither should any use of a moral test to determine if a message is truly from this being. But the use of this test shows that not all moral knowledge is dependent upon what is in a religion, just as it shows that all our knowledge of physics is not dependent on what is in a religion. Finally, no comparison of the content of physics and morality is being made, implied, or intended. We are, once again, considering a kind of argument, not the specific content of the subject matters of the arguments.

THE "DIRECTION"

Are actions right or wrong because God says they are, or does He say they are right or wrong because they are?[11] This is a distinction that is sometimes hard to get straight, but it is important in this discussion. When an umpire says "You're out!" the batter is thereby made out. There may be some fact in the world that we can appeal to and say the videotape shows the umpire made a mistake, but the baseball fact is that the batter is out. This is what goes into the official record book. It *becomes* a fact that the batter was out, and the judgment of the umpire brings that baseball fact into existence. In contrast with this is the judgment that the ball traveled 475 feet when hit by Canseco. This judgment is correct or not depending upon evidence gathered by measuring, not by the judgment of the Official Measurer. There is no Official Measurer, so any judgment I make about the distance is said to be correct or not depending upon whether I *have* measured accurately. I start at home plate and measure to the mark in the street made by the ball. There is some distance the ball went which one can correctly or incorrectly determine. When I say, "The ball flew 475 feet," this judgment does not bring the fact into existence. I claim that I am correct because the ball did travel 475 feet; it did not travel 475 feet because I say it did.

Are actions right or wrong because God says they are, or does He say they are because they are? To remind you, we are not talking here about whether God created the world or not. Let us suppose that God created the physical world just as it is, the one that has just these laws describing it. In the same way, God is supposed to have created all the laws of the world and of the relations of the creatures in it. This includes morality. Having made the world with its laws, God need not intervene to make it work properly. The earth rotates without God pushing it. At this moment the earth does not rotate because God judges "The earth rotates." He judges that the earth rotates because it does. His judgment does not create the present ongoing fact that the earth rotates. God judges that slavery is wrong but, in the same way and for the same reasons, God's judgment that slavery is wrong does not bring into existence the fact that slavery is wrong.

Some believe that God can work miracles in the physical world, for example, that He can stop the earth's rotation. He can suspend the way the world works and substitute other ways the world works. Some suppose that God could, in the same way, work moral miracles. For example, they think that God could, on occasion, make it

[11]This is the question Plato posed in his dialogue *Euthyphro*. In that work the heart of the argument presented in this section first appears.

happen that slavery is right. Other people, including your author, suppose that moral miracles are not possible for God because they would be contrary to his all-good nature. Moral miracle are, accordingly, no more possible than geometric miracles. God can no more make slavery in the U.S. in the eighteenth century or apartheid in South Africa right now than He could make a round square. Neither of these is something that is a possible action for God to do, it is claimed. Interesting though this is, we need not, fortunately, take a stand on this issue to continue our discussion.

There is a positive reason to suppose that moral notions, even if brought into existence by God, apply independently of God's judgment once they exist. To see this let us use the moral notion *good*. We say of people that they are good, not that they are right or wrong. "Socrates and Martin Luther King Jr. were good people" is an example. Religious people want also to say that God is good, indeed, the best being there is. If the view that God brings moral facts into existence by His judgment is correct, however, what this claim comes to is that God has judged of Himself that He is good. Religious people, though, want to say that it is God Himself who is good, not that He becomes good only because of a self-judgment. If it were a self-judgment, then, after all, God could be the creature some suppose exists, namely, a being who is evil incarnate. Were the universe to be run by a being whose aim is to cause the most suffering—as God's is to minimize suffering—and that being were to say of himself, "I am good," then he would *be* good. He would be good if we accepted the theory that the good of a being is created by the judgment of whoever created the universe. But, this is clearly not true. This being who is evil and not good does not become good by a self-pronouncement. To prevent this absurdity in our conceptual framework, we must reject the view that leads to it. The view that leads to it is that things are good because a being judges they are good.

Consider one last consequence of adopting the view that God's judgment creates the fact of goodness. Worshippers intend to say of God that He is good, that he has a certain character in virtue of which He is *worthy* of worship but the being who is evil incarnate is not. However, if the view we are considering is correct there is no (independent) notion of worth to which we can appeal. God's worth is a fact that He creates by his own judgment, not something that exists independently. So, those who are most religious would find that there is something they think is meaningful, namely, worshipping God because He is merciful, kind, and forgiving, that would be rendered not meaningful. These traits are totally irrelevant to God's goodness; only His self-appraisal is relevant. You might say "But perhaps all religious people are mistaken about God's nature and His role." Yes, this might be true. But if religious people are mistaken, then we are justified in rejecting the view that God does have such an "umpire's" role, for it was this religious view that generated this discussion. On the other hand, if they are correct about the nature of God, we are, for the reasons presented above, also justified in rejecting God as moral umpire. In either case, the view of God as moral umpire is one we are justified in rejecting. It is granted, of course, that religious people are the ones who have the most reason for rejecting the view that God is a moral umpire, for it would undermine their religion. For those who are not religious, this excursion has been of interest because so many people in our society are religious.

One topic I shall not discuss at any length is whether people would act in a morally acceptable way if they did not believe that a divine being would punish them if they did not. I do not think this is so, primarily because the moral lives of believers and nonbelievers seems not to be different. Many of those on death row are believers, and this is true of many rapists and others who act in morally heinous ways. This is not to say that the religious belief is responsible for the heinous behavior. It is well known that many of most morally exemplary people in history, Martin Luther King Jr., for example, were deeply religious. The only point here being made is that while religious belief does not cause the immoral actions, it apparently does not prevent them either. (Instructors may want to discuss this topic at greater length in class.)

EGOISM

Ethical egoism is the first NET we shall examine that has significant philosophical backing. Ethical egoism was defended in less clear forms by some ancient Greeks, but the view traces its modern roots to Thomas Hobbes (1588–1679), an English philosopher who set forth his version of ethical egoism. Hobbes set out his view most clearly in *Leviathan,* a work that gives the psychological and physical underpinnings of his ethical and political theory. Since Hobbes wrote *Leviathan,* other philosophers and many lay people have defended ethical egoism. In recent times the view has fallen out of favor with philosophers because of its many defects, though some still defend it. It is an ethical theory that does not go well with the perspective of most professions, as will be shown, but many within professions such as the military or medicine hold the view nevertheless. Finally, the view is still quite popular with students and many in the lay public, so it is worth setting out and evaluating.

TWO EGOISMS

There are two different views called egoism, one a theory of motivation and one a NET. The former is defended in ethics survey, item IV A and the latter defended in item V B. Following the usual custom, here is the NET, **ethical egoism,** as set out in the general scheme.

```
P1. If any action increases my own good, then it is right.
P2. Lying to my mother about how my birthday meal tastes
increases my own good.
Therefore, C. Lying to my mother about how my birthday meal
tastes is right.
```

As is true of the use of each of the NETs, the conclusion is a specific moral judgment. You may think that the second premise is false, but this is still how the theory works to arrive at specific moral judgments. An evaluation of the first premise interests us for now. Most who hold to ethical egoism follow Hobbes in trying to support it with a psychological theory of motivation called **psychological egoism.** Psychological egoism is a psychological theory of motivation, not a NET. A way to see how different the theories of ethical and psychological egoism are is to put psychological egoism in the same form as a NET (even though it is not a NET).

```
P1. If any action I perform is voluntary, then its motive
is to increase my own good.
P2. Lying to my mother about how my birthday meal tastes is
a voluntary action.
Therefore, C. The motive in lying to my mother about how my
birthday meal tastes is to increase my own good.
```

In the first argument the conclusion is a specific *moral* judgment, whereas in the second, the conclusion is a specific *motivational* judgment. The difference is crucial. The psychological theory is thought to provide support for the ethical theory, but they are different theories. The argument for the ethical theory can be stated very briefly using EE to stand for ethical egoism and PE to stand for psychological egoism.

```
P1. If PE, then EE.
P2. PE.
Therefore, C. EE
```

The justification for the first premise is subtle and complex in authors such as Hobbes, but one can get a clear idea of the basic position. If our only motive in acting voluntarily is to secure good for ourselves and this is a law of nature, then we cannot help but act in this way. A stone cannot help but fall; we cannot help but sweat if we exercise in warm weather; and no one can for long prevent the eyes from blinking. For all of those actions, we are permitted to do them because we cannot help but do them. Hobbes, noticing this and holding to PE, claimed, then, that we have a right to (that is, we are permitted to) act in our own benefit. This, most would agree, is a good inference. (We cannot infer that the action is right because it is permitted, but since there are other problems with the argument we will not worry about that for now.[12]) Since we are permitted to do what we cannot help but do, and we cannot help but act to secure our own benefit or good, then some version of EE would be established—if we could but establish PE. Unfortunately, PE is a seriously flawed theory of motivation.

---

[12]The action of drinking herb tea in the morning is permitted, but it is difficult to think of a circumstance in which it is right. Most actions that are permitted have no positive moral worth, so they are not morally right. Actions that are permitted are not obligatory either, for though I am permitted to drink herb tea, it is not obligatory. However, the notions of right and obligatory are ones that apply frequently; their use has to be accounted for. If one's NET could only account for the phenomena of permission it would be a poor candidate for best one.

PSYCHOLOGICAL EGOISM EVALUATED

There are undoubtedly more bad arguments constructed to support PE than any other view philosophers examine. Only a few of the more common ones will here be examined. Let us begin with the argument found in the ethics survey, item IV A. That argument, in a slightly different form, is

```
P1. If any action y of person A is voluntary, then A wants
to do y.
P2. If A wants to do y, then A's motive in doing y is to
satisfy the want.
P3. If A's motive in doing y is to satisfy a want, then A's
motive in doing y is self-benefit.
Therefore, C. If any action y of person A is voluntary, then
A's motive in doing y is self-benefit.
```

This is an unfamiliar argument form, but it is valid, so there is no problem with the logic of the argument. There are concerns, though, about the truth of the premises. The concern comes from an ambiguity of the term 'want.' In one sense it does get at desires, appetites, and other conditions that, when satisfied, benefit the person whose appetites they are. For example, when I drink water to satisfy my thirst, then it is I who am immediately benefited. Another sense of 'want', though, is a synonym for 'voluntary'. When I give to charity I do it voluntarily, in contrast to giving money to a thief who demands it. I usually do not have a desire or appetite to give to charity. In the first premise of the above argument, 'want' has to be used in the sense of desire or appetite in order for the premise to be about psychological egoism. If 'want' is used in the sense of voluntary action, the premise is true but useless for the psychological egoist. If the psychological egoist uses 'want' in the sense of desire or appetite in the first premise, though, an illegitimate assumption is being made. The assumption is illegitimate because the premise now assumes what was to be established by an argument, namely, that voluntary actions are driven by self-benefit (here, to satisfy passions or appetites). This is even clearer in P2, which tells us that voluntary action is done to fulfill wants or desires. This, though, is the point that the argument was going to establish. The assumption that this point—the point in contention—is correct is called begging the question. Nothing can be proved in this way, for any point could then be established.

Suppose I claim to be able to establish that life was created by a divine being. There are many arguments that attempt to establish this position, but one cannot use the claim that "all life has to be created by a divine being" as part of the evidence. This is another instance of begging the question. The clearest instance of begging the question, though, can be found in P3: The sense of 'want' as voluntary action in that premise simply states that voluntary action is performed to secure self-benefit. This is the very claim of psychological egoism![13]

[13]If we use 'want' in the desire/appetite sense, there is reason to think that P3 is false. Those who use tobacco, cocaine, or heroin can be said to pursue it from a passion or appetite, for they are addicted. However, it is clearly not to their self-benefit to use any of these harmful and addictive substances.

Supposing the above argument fails, though, there are others to examine. Here is another argument: "It is always possible that even when a person thinks an action is not done to secure self-benefit that it actually is. For example, people frequently open doors for strangers whose arms are full of packages. This seems to be a clear instance of doing something for someone else's benefit, not for self-benefit. But is it not *possible* that you would have felt guilty if you did not open the door? When people feel guilty, this is contrary to their self-benefit. So, opening the door actually was done to benefit yourself. The benefit is to avoid guilt." Sometimes, in this kind of argument, the benefit is supposed to be reciprocal action on the part of this person or others in the future, but that is not important here. What is important is the use of *possibility* in an attempt to establish the conclusion.

Possibility cannot be used to establish the conclusion because it can be used in exactly the same way on the other side. "You think you scratched your head because it would benefit you by relieving an itch. But, is it not possible that you did it because you would be unpleasant to others and be less productive on the job if your head continued to itch. So, scratching your head is done to benefit others." This is a bad argument, but it is as good as the one using possibility to support psychological egoism. The opposite extreme position—we can call it **psychological altruism** (PA), the view that all our voluntary actions are done to benefit others—is equally well supported by this argument. Our mythical psychological altruist would claim that this view is correct because it is possible that all our actions are done to benefit others. This argument, as is the one that purports to support psychological egoism, makes use of possibility to conclude something that is actually so. Since we agree this kind of argument cannot legitimately be used to support PA, it cannot legitimately be used to support PE. Any argument that can be used to support contrary positions is obviously not acceptable.

The reference to psychological altruism is a good lead-in to another frequently encountered argument, one whose first premise has a form that should look familiar.

```
P1. Either PE or PA is correct.
P2. PA is not correct.
Therefore, C. PE is correct.
```

The first premise of this argument offers two and only two options. Each of the options says there is only one source of motivation: PE says it is self-benefit, and PA says the benefit of others. Since I sometimes do things such as scratch an itch that primarily benefits me, actions whose motive is that very self-benefit, I and no doubt almost everyone would say that P2 is true. However, if there are other options besides these two extremes, the first premise is not acceptable. Since we can hold a position that recognizes some motives as directed to oneself and some directed to others, we would find the first premise unacceptable. This argument has the same flaw as the one that gives us the choice between ethical relativism and absolutism. The evidence leads us to reject the claim that there are just the two options.

In addition to rejection by philosophers, we find that psychological egoism is not a theory accepted by psychologists working in theory of motivation. Although it is not a very exciting view, the position that some of our motives are to benefit ourselves and some to benefit others seems to be what is true. This position, though, would show that the second premise of the argument with which we began is false. We began, recall, with the argument:

```
P1. If PE, then EE.
P2. PE.
Therefore, C. EE.
```

The second premise is not true, as our examination seems to show, so the argument is valid but not sound. The result is that the conclusion cannot be asserted on the basis of this argument. It does not imply that the conclusion is false, for EE might have other support. Let us, then, examine EE as we did ethical relativism and ethical absolutism, to see how it fares as an ethical theory.

ETHICAL EGOISM EVALUATED

Ethical egoism, as is true of any NET, has to show that it can explain the moral phenomena adequately. One typical criticism of EE is that it does not do that job very well. For example, if ethical egoism were correct, the keeping of slaves by Simon Legree in the eighteenth century would have been right. The action of the government of South Africa in keeping blacks disenfranchised is the right action of the overwhelming number of whites in that country. However, those actions are reasonably clear instances of actions that are not right. So, the NET, namely, EE, that gives the result that they are right is defective.

Any theory can account for the phenomena, but not every theory can *adequately* account for the phenomena. An ethical egoist might claim that it really does not benefit whites to continue the disenfranchisement of the black population. But, what reason is there to believe this other than a desire to save EE? It is one thing to make a claim and another to make a justified claim. Such claims, in response to these proposed counter-examples and many others like them, do not seem to have any independent support.

Another criticism of ethical egoism is that it has no way of reconciling or choosing between competing interests and benefits. It is to the benefit of someone who is in the white minority to keep the blacks in South Africa disenfranchised, but it is to the benefit of one of the black majority to have the vote. So, the same action is both right and wrong! A theory that allows contrary claims to be equally justified at the same time is surely mistaken.

Just as we saw the preference theory attempt to escape an inconsistency by bringing in the notion of *true for,* someone might attempt to use the same notion or the similar notion of *right for.* They might say that the actions are *right for* Simon Legree or any of the whites in South Africa and the actions are *wrong for* the slaves or any of the South

African blacks. Remember, though, this is just to say that each party believes the actions are right or wrong. Any NET that yields only judgments that contain 'believes is right' and not 'is right' is not a very good one. The aim of a NET is to yield *justified* singular moral judgments, not just judgments that are *believed to be* justified.

One reason this move to 'right for' might seem plausible and reasonable is that the notion of increasing good is in the second premise of each of the arguments that yields the contrary conclusions, and people might think of this in terms of being good for Simon Legree and bad for any of the slaves. This is a perfectly good way of speaking of the situation, and this is not a situation in which 'right for' is the same as 'believes.' Unfortunately for the defender of ethical egoism, it also does not escape the inconsistency. The good that accrues to Simon Legree is good in reality, not in his belief (alone). The bad the slaves suffer is not just evil in their beliefs, it is evil. They are forced to do work they do not want to do, their families are separated, they are beaten, sexually assaulted, and deprived of their freedom. Logically, each argument is a good one within ethical egoism, and so the inconsistency remains when we have arguments of the following sort, each from a different viewpoint:

```
P1. If any action increases my (Simon Legree's) overall
good, then it is right.
P2. Simon Legree's keeping slaves (including the one who
was named Eliza) increases my (Simon Legree's) overall good.
Therefore, C1. Simon Legree's keeping slaves is right.

P3. If any action decreases my (Eliza's) overall good, then
it is wrong.
P4. Simon Legree's keeping slaves (including me, Eliza)
decreases my good.
Therefore, C2. Simon Legree's keeping slaves is wrong.
```

The attempt to avoid the inconsistency must come in the consequent of the first premise so it appears in the conclusion of each argument. At that point we have two conclusions that are consistent, for then the arguments appear as follows:

```
P1. If any action increases my (Simon Legree's) overall
good, then it is right for Simon Legree.
P2. My (Simon Legree's) keeping slaves increases my overall
good.
Therefore, C3. Simon Legree's keeping slaves is right for
Simon Legree.

P3. If any action decreases my (Eliza's) overall good, then
it is wrong for Eliza.
P4. Simon Legree's keeping slaves (including me, Eliza)
decreases my good.
Therefore, C4. Simon Legree's keeping slaves is wrong for
Eliza.
```

The statements C3 and C4 are not contraries, though C1 and C2 are contraries. Why is this? Different people can believe contrary things and often do. Some believe that Iowa is larger than Michigan and others believe that Michigan is larger than Iowa. Now, it cannot be true that each is larger than the other, but two people can each have different beliefs about which one is larger. But this price of saving the theory from inconsistency is, as was true of the preference theory, too high. The purpose of a NET is to provide us with *justified* moral judgments, not just what we *believe* are justified moral judgments.[14]

Readers should keep in mind that ethical relativism, ethical absolutism, and ethical egoism each purport to be *the* correct normative ethical theory. Sometimes people do not realize this about NETs and think that combining two NETs will make up the deficiencies they see in each. The theories do not say they are presenting just one factor among many that determines that actions are right or wrong. For this reason, one cannot claim that both egoism and relativism are correct NETs. They each claim to be a complete and correct NET. It cannot be that the single factor that tells us whether an action is right is self-benefit and also that the single factor that tells us whether an action is right is what is accepted by the majority as right in that culture. We shall shortly examine a view, the variable-weight or prima facie theory, that does allow the use of many factors, but that is not the position of any of these views so far.

If we waive the difficulty of each theory purporting to be the correct NET, there are still insurmountable problems. It may be that on most occasions the two theories will give the same result. For example, both ethical relativism and ethical egoism will give the judgment that it is wrong to torture animals. However, on occasion the results will be different. For example, suppose someone will pay you a large sum of money to torture puppies in a film made for sadists. Relativism will yield the judgment that it is wrong to do it, but ethical egoism yields the view that it is right. There is nothing about either theory that tells you what to do when the two factors conflict. You may propose a fixed hierarchy of the rules—that ethical relativism is stronger than or overrides ethical egoism when the two conflict, a move that will not work either. It will not work because there are times when ethical relativism will have to yield to ethical egoism. For example, your friends all use tobacco and think that it is obligatory for anyone in their gang to use it. But it is not to your interest to do so. The issue of how to address a fixed hierarchy problem will be taken up in the next chapter in the discussion of a variable-weight NET. For now, though, you should note that a proposal simply to combine two of these NETs is not workable.

CONSCIENCE

"Let your conscience be your guide." We hear people talk about conscience a fair amount, and it is certainly part of our folklore. Conscience theories have had

---

[14]Of course, we do believe the judgments that are justified by the use of our (acceptable) NET, but the justification comes from the evidence in the argument, not from our belief. We all recognize that there is a big difference between a judgment that is believed without any evidence or perhaps even contrary to the evidence and one that is believed on the basis of good evidence.

defenders, so we shall briefly examine such a view. The conscience is typically thought of as a way of arriving at justified moral judgments in particular cases. The eyes are a way of arriving at judgments about the color of object, and reason is the way to decide about such matters as validity of arguments. In a similar way the conscience as a moral faculty is posed as the way to arrive at specific moral judgments. How would this work as a NET?

We could easily put the view into our usual form:

```
P1. If any action is judged by my conscience to be right,
then it is right.
P2. Action x is judged by my conscience to be right.
Therefore, C. Action x is right.
```

The major problem with this view is that different and equally sincere people report inconsistent judgments as the products of their respective consciences. One reports that her conscience tells her the U.S. should cease all trading with South Africa, while another reports that his conscience tells him that we ought to continue trading with South Africa. One says that abortion ought to be prohibited and the other that it is permissible. Both second premises cannot be true, for both conclusions cannot be true. How is this inconsistency to be avoided?

One way to avoid an inconsistency is to show that one of the applications of conscience was defective, for example, by providing evidence that trading with South Africa is, say, morally forbidden and not obligatory. But, if we can use some other method to arrive at such a specific moral judgment, then conscience is not the primary way of reaching such judgments. This "solution" to the problem of conflicting consciences would simply replace the theory with whatever method we used to decide whose conscience was correct.

Conscience is likely the name we give to our habitual way of arriving at specific moral judgments. People frequently are not consciously aware of how they arrive at decisions about many matters. For example, most people can adjust the force they use to hit a golf ball so as to get it to go a certain distance. This is not an incredibly precise adjustment, but most can do it reasonably well. When too great or too little force is used, the person sees the result and makes a correction. As a result of much practice, those who are good golfers can hit the ball more often than not with roughly the force they choose. Almost no one, though, can say how this is done. The same is true of estimating distance or any number of other skills. All of us have some method of arriving at specific moral judgments, but, as most of the readers are now aware, to be able to state that method in a clear manner is not easy. 'Conscience' may be a convenient name for that method, but if we take it seriously as a NET, it does not fare very well.

In the next chapter we shall examine views that are better than the ones examined so far. These are theories philosophers have spent more time and care on than most of the ones in this chapter. This does not mean they are perfect, but the flaws are more subtle and the defenses less obviously flimsy.

CHAPTER 3

Finalists

In the second chapter we examined theories so seriously flawed that they are unlikely to be in the final competition for best normative ethical theory. In this chapter we shall examine those theories that have withstood the test of criticism over a long period of time. These theories will, by and large, yield the same specific moral judgments, given agreement on the facts of a situation. There are still reasons to offer as to why one theory is better than the others, but the reasons are more subtle. After each of the theories is presented, the standard criticisms will be set out, and then, finally, a comparison of all the theories will be offered at the end of the chapter.

UTILITARIANISM

Earlier, we examined a sort of generic utilitarianism whose rule, as represented on the general scheme, is

        If any action increases overall good, then it is right.

This general form of utilitarianism allows us to contrast it with ethical egoism whose corresponding general rule is

        If any action increases my overall good, then it is right.

The theories agree in using *overall good* as the factor that determines right and wrong but disagree about whose good is to count. Egoism says it is those actions whose consequence increases *my* good that are right, whereas utilitarianism counts the consequences of actions for the good of *all*. Since both theories agree that the value of the likely consequences of actions determines right and wrong, they are called *consequentialist* theories.

CONSEQUENTIALIST THEORIES

Ethical egoism and utilitarianism both claim that moral terms such as 'right' or 'wrong' apply to proposed or actual actions, depending on the value of the likely or actual consequences of those actions.[1] Most of us would claim that vaccinating against measles is the right thing to do if the likely good to the entire population is greater than the likely harm to those few who will have an adverse reaction to the vaccination.[2] A small percentage of children have a serious reaction to the vaccination; there are even some deaths. However, when we consider the good that results, we judge that the program of vaccination is morally justified. If measles should be wiped out in the U.S. and Canada, and we are very close to that now, then we might no longer be justified in carrying out the program. Of course, there are other countries in which measles is still a common disease, so we might recommend a vaccination to those who travel abroad, even if we should eliminate measles in most of North America.

Some philosophers suppose that it is the likely or actual consequences of actions projected into the *indefinite future* that utilitarianism or any consequentialist theory must use to determine rightness. This is a bizarre form of consequentialism, however, for this makes the theory completely impractical. No one can calculate the consequences of actions into the next century, let alone for the next thousand years.[3] It is best to consider the consequences as we do in our everyday lives. Even though George Bush's birth was a consequence of his parents having sexual relations, his becoming president of the U.S. was not. It is certainly not a consequence of that sexual activity that one of Bush's children was swimming on a hot summer day in 1990. We can say, generally, that the *consequences of an action* are the *likely and important results of it, based on the evidence we could reasonably be expected to have*. The evidence clause makes it clear that unforeseeable consequences are not to be put into the calculation even later on. We are not justified on utilitarian grounds in saying that Stalin's parents did the wrong thing in having sexual relations because Stalin resulted from this action.

[1]To avoid further detailed discussion about the value of likely consequences or the likely value of consequences, the reader is to understand henceforth that when I talk about the consequences of actions, it is shorthand for the longer phrase concerning the *value* of the likely consequences of actions. When we get to chapter 4, Value, this discussion will be clearer.
[2]Once someone agrees with this reasoning, they must give up the view that human life is the only or greatest thing of intrinsic value. This claim will be taken up more fully in the next chapter on pp. 83–84.
[3]There are those who distinguish between a theory that can be *used as a way to determine* what is right or wrong and a theory that gives the *criterion* for what is right or wrong. They are inclined to think that one could hold that a theory is correct but useless in determining what is right or wrong. It is clear that I do not accept this view, and that if a theory were unable to apply to our moral problems and help us arrive at solutions, I would think that a very strong criticism of it.

GOOD

What *is* good is not here in question. You may think that only pleasure is good and pain bad, that only knowledge is good and ignorance bad, or that only freedom is good and slavery bad. You may think that all of these are good and that love, happiness (as a long-run state), courage, kindness, honesty, and many more things are good. The utilitarian must, sooner or later, tell us what things are good, but almost any theory about what is good can be plugged into the general principle that is utilitarianism. So, when you see 'good' or think of any of its synonyms such as 'value' or 'intrinsic value', keep in mind that no commitment to a specific theory of value has yet been made. Whatever good turns out to be, though, it is the good of all or the overall good that is talked about, not the overall good of one person.

Some philosophers have thought to limit those whose good counts to people at a location, a city, or country, but most have held that all humankind should be taken into account.[4] If creatures on this planet or others should turn out to be sufficiently sentient, then they too will have to be added to those whose good counts.

DIRECT AND INDIRECT UTILITARIANISM

So far, all the NETs examined apply directly to situations or actions. Their rules apply directly to those actions described in the second premise of the general scheme. However, the most influential forms of utilitarianism have been ones that applied primarily to rules that then apply directly to actions. The following statements should enable us to contrast the two versions:

```
P1. If any action increases overall good, then it is right.
P2. If any proposed direct moral rule, when generally acted
from, increases overall good, then it is a correct direct
moral rule.
```

The first rule will be called a **direct moral rule** because it applies directly to actions or situations. In contrast, the second rule is called an **indirect moral rule** because it applies to (direct) rules that then apply to actions or situations. However, those who are direct-rule utilitarians (or who are usually called *act utilitarians*) think we need only the direct rule. Those who are indirect-rule theorists (or who are usually called *rule utilitarians*) use many direct rules in their theory. The following quote from John Stuart Mill (1806–1873), the philosopher who has been the most influential utilitarian, shows that position in action. Mill is here responding to the criticism that since we do not have enough time to calculate the likely consequences of actions when we have to make moral judgments, utilitarianism is not a workable theory.

---

[4]We could construct numerous variations of utilitarian views based on the size of the group. For example, a view we might call nationalistic utilitarianism would look only to the likely good consequences as they concern the citizens of their own country. On occasion it might be useful to make such distinctions, but in this work there is no such need.

...there has been ample time, viz., the whole past duration of the human species. During all that time mankind have been learning by experience the tendencies of actions...mankind must by this time have acquired positive beliefs as to the effects of some actions on their happiness; and the beliefs which have thus come down are the rules of morality for the multitude, and for the philosopher until he has succeeded in finding better. The corollaries from the principle of utility, like the precepts of every practical art, admit of indefinite improvement, and, in a progressive state of the human mind, their improvement is perpetually going on. But to consider the rules of morality as improvable is one thing; to pass over the intermediate generalizations entirely and endeavor to test each individual action directly by the first principle is another. It is a strange notion that the acknowledgment of a first principle is inconsistent with the admission of secondary ones.[5]

In these passages we see Mill apparently holding to an indirect version of utilitarianism. Mill also, though, reserves the option of applying the principle of utility, the moral principle we have been looking at all this time, directly when there is a conflict between two direct or secondary rules. Let us see how this works. Suppose we have the following two direct moral rules (DMR stands for direct moral rule):

```
DMR1. If any action is one of lying, then it is wrong to do
it.
DMR2. If any action is one of preventing the hurting of
someone's feelings, then it is right to do it.
```

If we consider whether to lie to our mother about the special birthday meal she fixed, we can see that these two direct moral rules (DMRs) give us different and conflicting results: To lie to our mother is wrong, but to prevent a hurt to her (if we lie) is right. If all we had were the DMRs, the same action would be both right and wrong. Fortunately, to avoid the inconsistency, Mill tells us, "We must remember that only in these cases of conflict between secondary principles is it requisite that first principles should be appealed to."[6] Since this is a case of conflict, we would then apply the principle of utility directly to the situation, arriving, I think, at the judgment that it is right to lie and thus avoiding an inconsistency.

Students are sometimes puzzled about the origin of direct moral rules. Direct moral rules are the ones you learn at your parent's knee, read in sacred texts, hear in houses of worship, find in great works of literature, discover on your own, and get from morally wise people. It is moral progress to recognize that we need a DMR such as, "If any action consists of judging someone on the basis of race or sex, then it is wrong." This, as a DMR, gets added to our store of direct rules, and we teach it to our children. The new DMR, though, is not stronger in itself than any other DMR. We still need to use the procedure that Mill suggests if we would arrive at justified moral judgments.

[5]J. S. Mill, *Utilitarianism,* in *Utilitarianism,* ed. Samuel Gorowitz, (Indianapolis: The Bobbs-Merrill Company, Inc., 1971), p. 29. In his work Mill calls what I call here the principle of utility "the Greatest Happiness Principle." Custom has changed the wording, so I shall here follow contemporary custom.
[6]Mill, *Utilitarianism,* p. 30.

Some philosophers suppose that indirect or rule utilitarianism requires exceptionless direct rules. However, such exceptionless rules are absolutes, which rules we have found good reasons to reject. Secondly, the direct rules will conflict on occasion. If there is no way to reconcile the conflict within utilitarianism, then that theory is unworkable. Furthermore, there is no way to reconcile the conflict unless another rule is brought in. If the rule chosen is the principle of utility, then we have Mill's position. If the rule is something else, then we have given up utilitarianism. In light of this reasoning, the view of utilitarianism presented here is that of J. S. Mill. Since this view has been criticized severely in the past 125 years, we shall now look at the major criticisms that have been raised.

CRITICISMS

Without doubt, the most persistent criticism of Mill's view involves *justice*. The contemporary question of distributive justice concerns the morally proper way to distribute the things of value.[7] If the things of value are, for example, bags of wheat, we want to know how many bags of wheat we each ought to have. Many answers in the form of theories of distribution have been offered: according to need (communism), according to ability to compete in the market (capitalism), equally (egalitarianism), and according to merit (meritarianism). Mill and others in the nineteenth century conceived of justice in a wider sense, a sense that requires us to treat people with justice. However, Mill includes the sense that contemporary philosophers, political theorists, and economists use, so it is fair to have him answer our question about the morally proper way to distribute things of value. And answer it he does. Utilitarianism tells us to increase overall good, to aim for the most good we can get, but it does not tell us exactly how to reach that goal. The standard criticism of utilitarianism claims that if the most good we can get amounts to 100 units, then, on utilitarian grounds it makes no difference how we reach that 100. For example, one society might be the present one, and another, with exactly the same amount of good, might be a slave society. In one society there is a distribution according to ability to compete in the market place plus a "safety net" for those who are not able to do that, whereas in the latter a few live very well indeed, while most are slaves who do not live very well. Given the same amount of good in each then, *on utilitarian grounds,* there is no moral difference between the two societies. However, the argument concludes, since

---

[7]*Retributive* justice concerns punishment, that is, when and what kind of punishment is morally justified given a certain offense. This is a very important topic in social philosophy and social ethics, but we will not take it up here. Many are inclined to think that punishment is justified by citing retribution, but the utilitarian position is different. The utilitarians point out that punishment is designed to be something bad, or else it is not truly punishment. If we do something bad we need to justify it, for we are not thereby increasing the overall good. Certainly some good comes from the increased security that the rest of the citizens enjoy when we imprison a thief. However, that is not a very noticeable improvement in our lives, if noticeable at all. The positive good that results, say the utilitarians, must come from our *rehabilitating* the criminal who will then contribute to society.

Feelings of vengeance are quite natural for humans to experience when they are robbed or a loved one is assaulted. However, many natural feelings are ones we have an obligation not to act from. When one's small child awakens a parent in the middle of the night, it is natural to feel hostility, perhaps even a desire to inflict grievous physical harm. However, it is not morally permitted to act from this feeling. The utilitarians say the same thing about feelings of vengeance or the desire for revenge.

there is clearly a moral difference, utilitarianism does not do an adequate job in handling this crucial topic.

Mill was aware of this very criticism, a criticism which he addressed directly in chapter V of *Utilitarianism:* "On the Connection between Justice and Utility." In that chapter Mill surveys various senses of 'justice' current in English, which seem to be the same ones now current, and he attempts to show that his ethical theory can account for them and for the judgments made using them. The heart of the idea of justice involves "the idea of a personal right—a claim on the part of one or more individuals, like that which the law gives when it confers a proprietary or other legal right....Justice implies something which it is not only right to do and wrong not to do, but which some individual person can claim from us as his moral right."[8] A right—a RIGHT in my language—is something that others have an obligation to "defend me in the possession of."[9] What we ought to defend is, on Mill's view, determined by utility. We should distribute unequally, then, insofar as this will actually increase overall good. Furthermore, though this does not clearly apply directly here, each person's good is to count as much as anyone else's good. So, if my good is diminished in a certain social arrangement, that must be taken into account in calculating overall good.

> ...The entire history of social improvement has been a series of transitions by which one custom or institution after another, from being a supposed primary necessity of social existence, has passed into the rank of a universally stigmatized injustice and tyranny. So it has been with the distinctions of slaves and freemen, nobles and serfs, patricians and plebeians, and so it will be, and in part already is, with the aristocracies of color, race and sex.[10]

Are we ever justified in treating someone in an unjust way? Mill gives a qualified yes.

> ...to save a life, it may not only be allowable, but a duty, to steal or take by force the necessary food or medicine, or to kidnap and compel to officiate the only qualified medical practitioner. In such cases, as we do not call anything just which is not a virtue, we usually say, not that justice must give way to some other moral principle, but that what is just in ordinary cases is, by reason of that other principle, not just in the particular case.[11]

What about slavery? Mill would give his general answer, of course: Should we show that social utility is served by slavery, we would not call it a vice. However, Mill is adamant in claiming that slavery is never the way to maximize overall good. Slavery is, after all, economically inefficient. One does not get a lot of work out of those who have little to gain from it. Furthermore, the kinds of character traits we think are good, for example, kindness and diligence, are weakened by the institution of slavery. This is true of both the slave and the master. In a society in which slavery is dominant,

[8]Mill, *Utilitarianism*, pp. 49–50.
[9]Ibid., p. 50.
[10]Ibid., p. 56.
[11]Ibid., p. 57.

much less good will be generated than in a free society. We are more likely to increase the production of good of all sorts by using the intelligence, energy, and enterprise of all humans, not just a small part of society. For all these reasons, Mill would say that it is an empirical falsehood that we could ever have a slave society in which as much good was produced as would be produced with those same people in a free society.

Those who criticize Mill would respond that it is just a contingent or accidental fact that people are the way they are. As long as Mill's view allows even the possibility that slavery could be morally justified, then it is mistaken. The final response is that utilitarianism is a theory developed for humans as we know them, and, Mill would claim, it works better than any other theory for humans. There are those who want their NET to be not just true, but necessarily true. They require a NET to be true even if human beings should become pure thought. Utilitarianism would have to be changed somewhat if this were true, for what humans find good would no longer include bodily pleasures. But there is no guarantee that utilitarianism would be acceptable in its present form if humans changed in some other way we cannot now conceive. If someone is looking for a theory that would work no matter what humans turned out to be, then they had better present it, for no one has yet to do that. If Mill's theory should turn out to be the best NET, given human nature as it now is, that is good enough, surely, for humankind.

Many other standard criticisms of Mill have been answered in the course of setting out his view. For example, some say utilitarianism is unworkable because we do not have time to calculate the likely good consequences of each action. Another criticism is that some actions do increase overall good, but to such a small degree that they could not reasonably be called right. For example, suppose I scratch my nose, thereby relieving an itch. Even if this has no further consequences for anyone or anything else, scratching the itch does increase the total overall good by a very small amount. However, independently of utilitarianism, we know this is not a right action. This might be considered a cogent criticism of the direct (act) version of utilitarianism, but it does not apply to the indirect (rule) version. (What would the covering DMR be?)

A final criticism involves character and action. Since it is the value of the likely consequences of actions that alone determines what is right, the motive of the actor is irrelevant. But, some claim, the motives are sometimes relevant. For example, if someone gives to charity only for tax purposes, that action does not have positive moral worth. Mill, in response to this criticism, says that he is interested in good character, but that is a separate matter from the evaluation of actions.[12] There are some

---

[12]The law, as has been noted, reflects moral decisions we make. In the law a distinction is made among offenses on the basis of intention. Someone who kills his or her uncle by inadvertently giving him the wrong pill is guilty of, perhaps, negligent homicide but not murder. A charge of murder requires that the person intended the death of the uncle by giving him the pill. In the one case the action is morally wrong and in the other a tragic accident. The consequences, namely, the death of the uncle, are the same, but the moral quality of the action seems clearly to be different.

Mill would reply that the consequences are bad, but what covering DMR are we applying? Mill would not accept a DMR that said that any action that resulted in the death of another is wrong. It looks as though he would have to include motives and intentions in the DMR. But, then what are we to make of his claim that motives and intentions count only for goodness of character and that they have no connection to the evaluations of the actions of people? Perhaps Mill is talking about DMR utilitarianism when he makes his claim about the irrelevance of motives and intentions to the moral quality of actions.

right actions performed by persons of bad character from bad motives. If a person is, say, unkind, though, this will have a tendency finally to produce wrong actions. On Mill's view, a good character trait is one that tends to produce more good than its opposite. However, the full responses to these criticisms, if there be any, will not be attempted here. We have gone far enough in evaluating utilitarianism.

PRIMA FACIE/VARIABLE-WEIGHT THEORY

This theory, described in ethics survey, item III B, is a position finally endorsed by over 70% of those who have tried this ethics survey over the years. Furthermore, when people realize they do not have to accept either relativism or absolutism, they frequently adopt this theory. It may not be the first theory students adopt, but by the end of the term, given a presentation of the major views, the vast majority do adopt this view.

VARIABLE WEIGHT

A variable-weight NET is usually held as a direct moral rule (DMR) view. In chapter 1 the contrast between factors of variable weight and those of fixed weight was drawn. A fixed-weight factor is one that always has the same force, no matter what the situation, whereas a variable-weight factor varies in force from context to context. Since W. D. Ross is the philosopher who introduced 'prima facie' in the sense of factors of variable weight, let us see what he says about this notion.

> I suggest 'prima facie duty'…as a brief way of referring to the characteristic…which an act has, in virtue of being of a certain kind (e.g., the keeping of a promise), of being an act which would be a duty proper if it were not at the same time of another kind which is morally significant. Whether an act is a duty proper or actual duty depends on all the morally significant kinds it is an instance of…what I am speaking of is an objective fact involved in the nature of the situation, or more strictly in an element of its nature, though not, as duty proper does, arising from its whole nature.[13]

Since 'prima facie' is a shorter phrase than 'variable weight' and since the term is in current philosophical use, that is phrase we will use. But we must make it clearer, especially since we will not be working within Ross' general philosophical framework. The best way to make the notion clearer is to contrast it with two other notions, *categorical* and *actual*.

PRIMA FACIE—CATEGORICAL AND ACTUAL

'Prima facie,' as used of duties (or obligations or right actions), contrasts with two different notions. The first of these is **categorical.** A factor is taken categorically in a rule, which is accordingly a categorical rule, when *once it*

[13]W. D. Ross, The Right and the Good (Oxford: Oxford University Press, London, 1930), pp. 19, 20.

applies, the action is obligatory no matter what else is true of it. For example, let us suppose the rule "If any action is one of telling the truth then it is obligatory" is categorical. When this rule is taken as categorical, even if the action is also one of hurting someone's feelings for no real purpose, or one that results in the death of the person to whom you tell the truth, your obligation continues to be to tell the truth. In contrast, a rule taken as **prima facie** is one that admits the relevance of other factors. In addition to *truth telling,* in this situation the factor *avoiding hurting people's feelings* applies. You first determine if the action is an instance of both of those factors (and any others) in order to determine if your actual obligation is to tell the truth or not. If telling the truth would hurt someone's feelings, as would be true if you told your mother you thought the special meal she made for your birthday was awful, then you must decide which of the factors/rules is *weightiest* in that set of circumstances. Having made that decision you have then decided what your **actual** obligation is.

For those who suppose there are categorical rules, any time one applies it establishes an actual obligation. If your rules are of variable weight, though, you cannot tell whether you have an actual obligation from knowing that just one factor applies. In those circumstances, it is appropriate to say that you have a prima facie obligation even if you do not have an actual obligation. Within a prima facie theory, the actual obligation is determined by finding all the factors that apply, that is, all the prima facie rules that apply, and then determining which one or combination of these is weightiest in a given set of circumstances.[14] Categorical rules are absolutes. We have given reasons to suppose that there are no such rules, but we will have to reopen this discussion in the next section when we discuss Kant's theory. For now, we want an understanding of what prima facie rules are.

HOW MANY FACTORS?

Is there a specified number of moral factors? Ross thought he had discovered all there were, but he left it open that others may be found in the future. The factors he mentions are

    i. Promises.
   ii. Reparation for wrong deeds done.
  iii. Gratitude for services rendered to me by others.
   iv. Prevention of reward to those who do not deserve it.
    v. Good that can be brought about.
   vi. Self-improvement
  vii. Prevention of bad or harm to others.

[14]The prima facie rules are DMRs. The secondary rules of Mill are also DMRs. What is the difference, then, between the two theories? What makes Mill a utilitarian is that the principle of utility is the device to decide the relative weightiness of competing DMRs. What device is available for a prima facie theory? We shall see, but that is certainly one of the problems for this kind of theory.

Each of these can be put into our familiar form to get a prima facie rule of obligation. For example, "If any action increases good, then it is prima facie obligatory," is a way of putting factor v above into a prima facie rule. This prima facie DMR is not the principle of utility, since the other principles are equally prima facie principles. It is sometimes called the principle of beneficence. Each of these factors is stated positively, but each has a negative version. For example, doing harm to someone is prima facie forbidden or obligatory not to do. "If any action causes harm or decreases good, then it is prima facie forbidden (obligatory not to do)." You should try your hand at this kind of translation to make sure you know how each factor would enter into a prima facie rule.

CRITICISMS

Many of the criticisms of a prima facie theory are directed to the specific version of it held by Ross. For utilitarianism we tied the view to Mill as the one who was most influential and still has, in my opinion, the best version of it. But, because of insurmountable difficulties with Ross' intuitionist view, we shall not tie a prima facie theory to its originator.

One criticism of Ross is that he is an intuitionist. He claims that each of the prima facie rules is self-evident.

> What comes first in time is the apprehension of the self-evident prima facie rightness of an individual act of a particular type. From this we come by reflection to apprehend the self-evident general principle of prima facie duty.[15]

When we ask about self-evidence, we find that what one person says is self-evident another will reject. Some think it is self-evident that the races ought not to "mix," whereas some think that human races differ only superficially. Self-evidence is an elevation of one person's opinion to the status of an axiom (as the American philosopher C. S. Peirce pointed out). Self-evidence smacks of faculty psychology, the positing of various senses such as moral faculties and special faculties by which we are aware of physical objects to account for our knowledge of the world. Such views are no longer current in psychology or philosophy, and if the prima facie theory rested on them, we should also reject it. However, we do not have to rest a prima facie theory on intuition or on the claim that the principles are self-evident. We can, instead, propose it as a NET aiming to explain the moral phenomena and to help us arrive at specific moral judgments. We can then compare the job it does as a NET with the job that its rivals such as utilitarianism, kantianism, and a virtue-ethics theory do. In this

---

[15]Ross, *The Right and the Good*, p. 33. This is a somewhat puzzling passage, but it can be explained without getting in too deep. H. A. Prichard, *Moral Obligation* (London: Oxford University Press, 1957), was the author who most influenced Ross here. It was Prichard's view that we were directly aware, by a kind of intuition, that specific actions were obligatory. He also said, though, that it was in virtue of an action's being of a kind such as promising that we had this direct knowledge. Ross seems in this passage to be following Prichard in saying we have direct knowledge of the rightness of an action, but that this leads to direct awareness of the *kind* of action being right. This awareness of a kind of action being right is the direct knowledge of a principle.

way, we can avoid the objectionable theory of knowledge that Ross presupposed in his own version of the theory. But even so, there are serious problems.

The most serious problem facing a prima facie theory concerns the weighing procedure. Suppose there are two people who agree that all the factors that Ross mentions are indeed factors and that two of the factors apply in a given situation. We shall, for a change of pace, choose a few different principles.

```
PF1. If any action is an instance of breaking a promise,
then it is prima facie obligatory not to do.
PF2. If any action is an instance of increasing good, then
it is prima facie obligatory to do.
```

Suppose you are a physician who has promised the family of a patient to do everything you can to keep that patient alive. Suppose further that the patient has permanent brain damage resulting in a permanent loss of consciousness. The family members of the patient suffer continued anxiety and are distressed from seeing their loved one in this state. The expense of continued care is draining the resources of the family. You can, as a physician, code the patient so that in case of respiratory failure the staff will not resuscitate. If you do this, though, you violate the first rule. If you do not do this, you violate the second rule. You must, accordingly, decide which of the two rules is weightier.

The rules conflict as prima facie rules, but—since prima facie rules allow competing factors—there is no (logical) inconsistency. The same action, coding for nonresuscitation, is prima facie obligatory to do and prima facie obligatory not to do. It can, at most, be only actually obligatory to do one of those actions. But supposing it is one: Which one? You are to decide by deciding which rule or factor is weightiest in this set of circumstances. But how does one do that? Mill, recall, used the principle of utility to decide between competing secondary or direct moral rules. Ross, however, has no indirect moral rule to use to choose between competing prima facie rules (which are direct moral rules). What would be wrong, you might ask, in choosing such an indirect rule?

There *is* a problem in choosing such an indirect rule, for we must ask whether that indirect rule is itself categorical or prima facie. If it is categorical[16] it could settle the question but only at great expense to the theory. The categorical indirect moral rule (CIMR) might be as follows:

```
CIMR. If any two prima facie rules conflict, then the order
of precedence is always: PF1 > PF5, PF2 > PF3, and so forth.
```

[16]The same problem exists if the rule is of *fixed weight*. If there is one such rule then it is, of course, categorical since nothing else can override it. When there are two or more such fixed-weight indirect rules, then each one will set out a fixed hierarchy of precedence, as is indicated above. One such rule might say, "PF1 > PF2," and another that one is higher in the indirect hierarchy of the direct moral rules. If there is a fixed hierarchy, though, the theory ceases to be a prima facie or variable-weight NET. Each rule will represent an absolute, though, now by means of the indirect-weighing rules. Such a theory, as has been shown in chapter 2, is unacceptable.

This rule will not do, for it is incompatible with the prima facie theory itself. The most attractive part of a prima facie theory is that there is no set weight to the many factors, there is no fixed hierarchy. The reason this is attractive is that, in explaining the moral phenomenon, it recognizes that on some occasions one factor outweighs a second, but on other occasions the second outweighs the first. This proposed solution would eliminate that feature of the theory, a feature that is essential to its being the kind of theory it is.

You might suggest we use the principle of utility as the indirect moral rule, but that would then simply be to transform the prima facie theory into indirect (rule) utilitarianism. This is not to save a theory but rather to give it up. The solution to the problem must not result in a different theory; otherwise it is not a solution to the problem of that theory.

Why not say what a respected philosopher, William K. Frankena says?

> ...I am forced to conclude that the problem of conflict that faced the pluralistic deonto-logical theories discussed earlier is still with us. One can only hope that, if we take the moral point of view, become clearheaded, and come to know all that is relevant, we will also come to agree on ways of acting that are satisfactory to all concerned.[17]

This, though, seems simply to give up any explanation of the procedure. If we can agree on ways of acting that are satisfactory to all, then we do not need the prima facie theory—or any theory. We turn to NETs because there are moral problems we have difficulty solving. If, in an attempt to respond to the criticism that we do not know how to solve a crucial problem with our theory, you tell us that we maybe will agree on our moral judgments, we will have returned to the beginning. This, then, is no solution to the problem.

We are left with a very serious problem with a prima facie theory, though it seems to be true that we agree most of the time. Those who wish to use anything like variable-weight factors need a method for resolving conflicts. I have used a method that seems to do that, but instead of presenting it here, it is better to direct you to the appendix which contains a description of a method of selecting the factors that are weightiest and thus of arriving at specific moral judgments. This method, *moral negotiation,* is usable with any NET, but it fits particularly well with a view that employs a number of variable-weight factors.

KANT

Immanuel Kant (1724–1804) was one of the most influential thinkers of the eighteenth century. He made significant contributions in science as well as philosophy. Unfortunately, he wrote in a difficult academic style that makes his work

---

[17]William K. Frankena, *Ethics,* 2nd ed. (Englewood Cliffs, NJ: Prentice-Hall, 1973), p. 53. By 'deontological' Frankena contrasts those NETs that admit only consequences as factors (utilitarianism and ethical egoism) with those theories that allow factors in addition to consequences, since Ross allows promise keeping and other non-consequentialist factors he is a deontologist. Someone such as Kant who included only nonconsequentialist factors is called a formalist.

less accessible to a general public than it deserves to be. His ethical theory has influenced many contemporary thinkers, so it is worth examining closely. Kant's theory seems to have two quite different parts, one purely formal and the other a substantive principle. Kant thinks the two are really the same, but I shall try to show that this is not plausible.

THE CATEGORICAL IMPERATIVE

Kant held an indirect moral rule theory, as did Mill. Kant called his indirect moral rule the *categorical imperative*. This rule and how it is supposed to work can be seen in the following passage:

> An action done from duty has its moral worth, not in the purpose to be attained by it, but in the maxim in accordance with which it is to be decided upon; it depends, therefore, not on the realization of the object of the action, but solely on the principle of volition in accordance with which, irrespective of all objects of the faculty of desire, the action has been performed. That the purposes we may have in our actions, and also their effects considered as ends and motives of the will, can give to actions no unconditioned and moral worth is clear from what has gone before. Where then can this worth be found if we are not to find it in the will's relation to the effect hoped for from the action? It can be found nowhere but in the principle of the will, irrespective of the ends which can be brought about by such an action...
>   But what kind of law can this be the thought of which, even without regard to the results expected from it, has to determine the will if this is to be called good absolutely and without qualifications? Since I have robbed the will of every inducement that might arise for it as a consequence of obeying any particular law, nothing is left but the conformity of actions to universal law as such, and this alone must serve the will as its principle. That is to say, I ought never to act except in such a way that I can also will that my maxim would become a universal law. Here bare conformity to universal law as such (without having as its base any law prescribing particular actions) is what serves the will as its principle, and must so serve it if duty is not to be everywhere an empty delusion and a chimerical concept. The ordinary reason of mankind also agrees with this completely in its practical judgments and always has the aforesaid principle before its eyes.[18]

This is the formal part of Kant's theory. It gives us a NET with the indirect moral rule called the categorical imperative. The indirect moral rule is, in our form:

```
P1. If any proposed maxim (DMR) can be willed to be a
universal law of nature, then it is a correct maxim (DMR).
P2. "If any action is one of lying, then it is forbidden
(obligatory not to do)" is a proposed maxim (DMR) that can
be willed to be a universal law of nature.
Therefore, C. "If any action is one of lying, then it is
forbidden" is a correct maxim (DMR).
```

[18]Immanuel Kant, *The Moral Law: Kant's Groundwork of the Metaphysics of Morals*, trans. and analyzed by H. J. Paton (New York: Harper & Row, 1964) pp. 67–70. (Originally published by London: Hutchinson University Library, 1948).

One would then use the DMR to arrive at a moral judgment in a particular case. Let us first see how Kant shows his theory at work and then put it into our familiar form.

> Suppose I seek, however, to learn in the quickest way and yet unerringly how to solve the problem 'Does a lying promise accord with duty?' I have then to ask myself 'Should I really be content that my maxim (the maxim of getting out of a difficulty by a false promise) should hold as a universal law (one valid both for myself and others)?' And could I really say to myself that everyone may make a false promise if he finds himself in a difficulty from which he can extricate himself in no other way?' I then become aware at once that I can indeed will to lie, but I can by no means will a universal law of lying; for by such a law there could properly be no promises at all, since it would be futile to profess a will for future action to others who would not believe my profession or who, if they did so over-hastily would pay me back in like coin; and consequently my maxim, as soon as it was made a universal law, would be bound to annul itself.
>
> Thus I need no far-reaching ingenuity to find out what I have to do in order to possess a good will. Inexperienced in the course of world affairs and incapable of being prepared for all the chances that happen in it, I ask myself only, 'Can you also will that your maxim should become a universal law?' Where you cannot, it is to be rejected, and that not because of a prospective loss to you or even to others, but because it cannot fit as a principle into a possible enactment of universal law.[19]

The universal law in this instance is the proposed maxim (DMR). Such a proposed maxim and how it would work in a typical piece of moral reasoning made explicit might be:

```
P1. If any action is an instance of lying (making a false
promise) to get out of a difficulty, then it is morally
permitted (that is, not obligatory not to do).
P2. Lying to my creditors about now having the money in the
bank to cover a check just wrote to pay off my debts is an
instance of lying to get out of a difficulty.
Therefore, C. Lying to my creditors about now having money
in the bank to cover a check just wrote to pay off my debts
is morally permitted.
```

This is how the proposed maxim (DMR) would work if it were acceptable as a maxim. I know that I can get the money into my account before the check clears, but it is not in the account now. When I write the check, I will receive more goods from my creditors, goods for which I already have a buyer. With the proceeds from that sale I will cover the check already written to my creditors. Thus I would get out of a financial difficulty by making a false promise. This is how the maxim would work if it were acceptable, but is it acceptable? In the passage cited, Kant argues that it is not because it would not be an acceptable second premise in an argument that has the categorical imperative as the indirect moral rule in the first premise.

[19]Ibid., pp. 70–71.

P1. If any proposed maxim (DMR) can be willed to be a universal law of nature, then it is a correct maxim (DMR).
P2. "If any action is an instance of lying (making a false promise) to get out of a difficulty then it is morally permitted (not obligatory not to do)," is a proposed maxim (DMR) that can be willed to be a universal law of nature.
Therefore, C. "If any action is an instance of lying (making a false promise) to get out of a difficulty, then it is morally permitted" is a correct maxim (DMR).

Kant claims that the second premise in the above argument is not true. But we have to understand why he thinks the premise is false. He does not think that it is false because, as Mill claims he holds, it would have bad consequences for everyone to lie. Recall, Mill's position is that the secondary rules, the DMRs, are acceptable if generally acting on them increases overall good. In effect, this is the position he says that Kant actually holds, in spite of what Kant says he is doing. Kant would agree that if people generally lied there would be a breakdown in trust which would decrease overall good. This, though, is a utilitarian consideration, a consideration that Kant rejects. Remember, Kant says, "Where you cannot, it is to be rejected, and not that because of a prospective loss to you or *even to others* but because it cannot fit as a principle into a possible enactment of universal law." (I have added the emphasis here to show that Kant is rejecting a utilitarian account of the rejection.) Mill might be correct in suggesting that Kant is covertly appealing to the principle of utility, but we shall interpret Kant as holding a unique view.

Those who agree with Kant think he is making a logical point, so we shall try to generate such a point. When I promise to pay back the money by writing a good check, I need to have those to whom I make the promise accept it. If they did not accept it, then I would thereby be ruined. This is to say, in Kant's framework, that in making the promise I have universalized the proposed maxim (DMR) "If any action is an instance of telling the truth, then it is obligatory to do it." In its negative form this would be "If any action is an instance of lying then it is forbidden (not morally permitted) to do it." My creditors must suppose this maxim in order for them to accept my check. But, then, I am willing this maxim, and I am also willing its negation. I am willing both that it is permitted to lie and that it is forbidden to lie. It is forbidden because that is what I must will in order to get my money. It is forbidden because that is the way I do will that others should deal with me. It is permitted because I have also promulgated the maxim that it is permitted in this particular case involving me. So, I am caught in a contradiction when I attempt to will the maxim that making a lying promise is permissible. This shows, says Kant, that the action that falls under the maxim is not justifiably claimed to be permissible. Since the maxim that prohibits lying *is* universalizable, I can consistently will it, since no contradiction follows from willing it, and so my duty or obligation is to tell the truth. This, I think, is a clear way to show how there might be a logical problem in trying to legislate, as Kant sometimes says, certain maxims (DMRs).

However, most philosophers do not think there is any contradiction. It is generally thought that the maxim "If any action is one of my making an exception in my own case to the otherwise universal maxim prohibiting lying, then that is permitted" is universalizable. If someone does not like this form they can try "If anyone has fingerprints xyz (where this uniquely describes me), then that person is permitted to make a lying promise when it would rescue that person from financial difficulty." This maxim gets me out of the logical contradiction, and so would permit the lying promise that Kant wants to rule out. A related criticism is that one could universalize all manner of behaviors that have nothing to do with morality. The maxim "If any action consists of tying one's left shoe before the right, then it ought to be done" seems clearly universalizable. However, tying the left shoe before the right is not a duty; it typically has no moral significance at all. Since all these maxims appear to be acceptable, Kant's theory allows too much into the moral sphere. Are these criticisms correct? The reader will have to carry on here, for it would take us too far afield in this work to say more about this criticism. We must now examine another part of Kant's view that is important and has been more influential than the formal part described above. This is the part that concerns treating people as ends only and not merely as means.

KINGDOM OF ENDS

The notion of a kingdom of ends has been very influential, though how it works in relation to the categorical imperative is not clear. First, let us see what Kant has to say about this notion.

> For rational beings all stand under the law that each of them should treat himself and all others, never merely as a means, but always at the same time as an end in himself. But by so doing there arises a systematic union of rational beings under common objective laws—that is, a kingdom. Since these laws are directed precisely to the relation of such beings to one another as ends and means, this kingdom can be called a kingdom of ends (which is admittedly only an Ideal).
>
> The practical necessity of acting on this principle—that is, duty—is in no way based on feelings, impulses, and inclinations, but only on the relation of rational beings to one another, a relation in which the will of a rational being must always be regarded as making universal law, because otherwise he could not be conceived as an end in himself. Reason thus related every maxim of the will, considered as making universal law, to every other will and also to every action towards oneself; it does so, not because of any further motive or future advantage, but from the Idea of the dignity of a rational being who obeys no law other than that which he at the same time enacts himself.
>
> ...that which constitutes the sole condition under which anything can be an end in itself has not merely a relative value—that is, a price—but has an intrinsic value—that is, dignity.
>
> Now morality is the only condition under which a rational being can be an end in himself; for only through this is it possible to be a law-making member in a kingdom of ends. Therefore, morality and humanity so far as it is capable of morality, is the only thing which has dignity.[20]

[20]Ibid., pp. 101, 102.

One way of understanding these passages is indeed by way of the notion of *intrinsic value*, but it is difficult then to see this as part of the same mechanism as the categorical imperative. Each of us is capable of determining how properly to live in an independent way. We do this by deciding how to act on the basis of maxims or direct moral rules. Those creatures who do this are members of the kingdom of ends, creatures who are self-governing rather than mere followers of what others (or their instincts) decide. Slavery, for example, is immoral because it robs people of what is of the greatest value, namely, their worth as human beings. To deprive someone of their dignity is to prevent them from using their capacity to be self-governing. When we exercise this dignity, we are thereby, to use Kant's term, exercising our autonomy. This suggests a substantive moral principle, itself a maxim or direct moral rule:

```
If any action consists of respecting a person's dignity,
then it is obligatory to do.
If any action consists of violating a person's dignity, then
it is forbidden.
```

Kant does not think these are maxims or direct moral rules to be approved by the categorical imperative; he thinks that dignity is another way of stating the one moral law. While there are scholars who think that this is so, most philosophers are inclined to think that when he talks about dignity Kant has asserted a direct moral rule with some content, not just a formal requirement for legislating other moral rules. It seems to me that this latter position is correct, though it would not affect the criticism of the formal (universalizability) part of Kant's theory. The moral rule is one that most of us would be sympathetic with, for autonomy is something we are inclined to agree is of intrinsic value. When, for example, we support the aim of the elderly to live by themselves and not to enter nursing homes, we are opting for autonomy. When we claim that motorcycle-helmet laws ought not to be passed and argue about the moral permissibility of mandatory seat belt laws, we are appealing to autonomy.[21] This rule of autonomy, taken as a direct moral rule, must then be examined.

Is the direct moral rule of autonomy, as Kant seems to suggest, itself a categorical moral rule? Is it, in the sense here introduced, a moral absolute? The argument that it is not is by now a familiar one. We are sometimes justified in restricting a person's autonomy, sometimes for the common good and sometimes, though rarely, for that person's own good. We prohibit you, in North America, from driving on the left hand side of the road, for our good and yours too. This seems to be a clear instance of justifiably overriding your autonomy. We can endorse the moral rule of autonomy (or dignity) as a strong prima facie or variable-weight rule but not as an absolute. We shall better understand what Kant is saying about intrinsic value when we turn to theory of value in the next chapter, where we shall get clearer about the nature of value and inquire into what theory of value, if any, is justified.

---

[21]When we act for someone else's good without that person's permission, and often against the wishes of that person, we call that *paternalism*. Kant would claim that paternalism toward adults who are rational is not morally permitted. This is still a controversial position.

RIGHTS

Another outlook in contemporary ethical theory that looks to Kant for support is the view that the primary notion in ethics is RIGHTS. Such people think of Jefferson's claim in the Declaration of Independence that all people have certain "inalienable" RIGHTS, and that among them are "life, liberty, and the pursuit of happiness." The position of Jefferson is derived from the political theory of John Locke who thought that the (one) basic RIGHT was a property RIGHT. We all, in a sense, own our own body, and so anyone who tries to enslave us or otherwise force us to do what we do not choose to do is violating our property RIGHT in ourselves. This view is not needed, of course, to hold a RIGHTS-oriented view of morality.

RIGHTS generate obligations on the part of others to do or not to do something. We have an obligation not to kill Jefferson because he has a life RIGHT. Most of the RIGHTS conceived by philosophers and political theorists are negative, that is, they generate obligations on the part of others not to do something. Life and liberty RIGHTS would generate, respectively, obligations not to kill and not to interfere with the actions others choose to do. When a person acts on self-chosen maxims, that person is, to use Kant's phrase, acting autonomously. When we do not interfere with a person's actions, we are allowing the person the exercise of dignity. Treating someone with dignity and recognizing a liberty RIGHT would then be the same thing.

A RIGHTS-based NET would be one that posited some number of RIGHTS that are true of each person.[22] The following are among the more popular RIGHTS that people posit:

1. Life
2. Liberty
3. Privacy
4. Autonomy (if different from liberty).

In addition to the negative RIGHTS, some people posit a number of positive RIGHTS, or RIGHTS that would generate obligations on the part of others to do something. For example, a job RIGHT, if a person had one, would generate an obligation on the part of some others to provide employment. Some people argue that in order for people to exercise their freedom or their dignity, they need to have work that gives satisfaction and a sense of accomplishment. The same is said of a proposed health care RIGHT, a proposed positive RIGHT that would generate an obligation on the part of health professionals and the rest of us to provide health care to those in need of it. Certainly we want to have some rational set of proposed RIGHTS, or else we will have no way to resist claims such as that people have a smoking tobacco RIGHT.

---

[22]The assumption will be that we are talking about adults who are reasonably rational agents. It is not an easy task to say what it is to be a rational agent, but those who have enough intelligence to care for their needs and who typically aim at ends that are reasonably understood as good would be rational.

While it is not plausible to maintain there is a smoking RIGHT, it is plausible to say that to prevent someone from smoking when that smoking hurts no one else is to violate that person's autonomy or privacy RIGHT. That is, the autonomy RIGHT generates an obligation on the part of others not to interfere with someone's action of smoking. So, on the RIGHTS-based theory under consideration, it will be supposed that there is some small number of negative RIGHTS, from which obligations to do or to abstain from doing are generated. There may be some additional small number of positive RIGHTS, but this is a more controversial claim.

Each of the RIGHTS and their generated obligations will be interpreted as variable in weight or prima facie. So, though someone has a life RIGHT, on this theory, the obligation not to kill can be overridden by another obligation (or RIGHT). If a sniper is actively shooting people from a vantage point and refuses to surrender, the police sharpshooter has a prima facie obligation not to shoot and also a prima facie obligation to shoot. In this kind of case the actual obligation is to shoot the sniper, knowing the likelihood is that the sharpshooter will kill the sniper.

Insofar as the list of prima facie obligations and the sources of RIGHTS are the same, we have two theories that are equivalent. This would not be the case if someone held a theory of an absolute RIGHT, a right whose obligation to do or not to do could not be overridden. However, all the arguments already presented against such a theory would be fatal to an absolutist RIGHTS view.

Sometimes people talk about others "losing" RIGHTS. They say that criminals lose their freedom or life RIGHT. This is a misleading way of talking, since we can more accurately say the RIGHTS are overridden by other RIGHTS or obligations. So, we will not describe the situation by saying that anyone has lost a RIGHT.

Mill thought that RIGHTS and obligations were *correlatives*. He thought, of course, that *obligation* was the basic moral notion, explained by the Greatest Happiness principle. Once we have obligations, though, we can say the obligations generate RIGHTS on the part of others to do or not to do something. Once we begin to talk about RIGHTS, we can use that notion to justify our claim of obligations. Put in this way, Mill is seen as someone who has an obligation-centered NET in contrast to a RIGHTS-oriented approach. Which approach is better?

One consideration is that we have some agreement on the sources of obligation, but there is little agreement on RIGHTS. People seem to posit RIGHTS whenever they wish to make a moral judgment. Some people, for example, think that raising their children as they choose is a RIGHT. This is used to justify not seeking medical treatment for ill children. Of course, some RIGHTS are protected in the U.S. Constitution, so people often find this a natural way to talk. However, the RIGHTS mentioned in the Constitution, for example, freedom of speech, were protected because most Americans were convinced that people "naturally" had these RIGHTS. The RIGHTS are *protected* by law, not *created* by law.

If I had my choice, I would declare a moratorium on RIGHTS talk because of the abuse and the unclarity that often result from the use of this notion. Since I do not have a choice, my hope is to influence a restriction on the number of

RIGHTS and to indicate how the notions work in a NET. Since no really new theory results from the introduction of RIGHTS, nothing more need be said, and we can turn to another commonly used device in contemporary ethical theory, namely, contractarianism.

CONTRACTARIANISM FROM HOBBES TO RAWLS

A view that began as a theory to explain the legitimate power of the state has been used in recent times to provide a base for a normative ethical theory. In the U.S. Declaration of Independence we find Jefferson claiming that

> ...all Men are created equal, that they are endowed by their Creator with certain unalienable Rights, that among these are Life, Liberty, and the Pursuit of Happiness— That to secure these Rights, Governments are instituted among Men, deriving their just Powers from the Consent of the Governed.

Jefferson is here echoing the English philosopher John Locke, from whose works Jefferson borrowed the view that a government is justified in exercising power over citizens only when those citizens have explicitly or implicitly given the government that power. It is assumed on this view that RIGHTS belong to individual persons and that any RIGHTS held by the state are "given" to it by individuals because of certain advantages of living in a social rather than in a solitary manner. This view is stated early on by Plato in *Republic* and is given a more elaborate treatment by Thomas Hobbes in the seventeenth century. Perhaps the clearest statement of the source of the legitimate power of the state comes from the nineteenth-century American writer, Henry David Thoreau. Speaking of the legitimate power of the state, he says:

> It can have no pure right over my person and property, but what I concede to it. The progress from an absolute to a limited monarchy to a democracy, is a progress toward a true respect for the individual....There will never be a really free and enlightened state until the state comes to recognize the individual as a higher and independent power, from which all its own power and authority are derived and treats him accordingly.[23]

In this passage Thoreau captures a popular American and British view that basic RIGHTS are held by individuals and then, in some transfer of legitimate authority, the state is given some of these RIGHTS. How does this transfer take place, and what is the motive? The transfer is done by an agreement, a contract or compact into which individuals enter because it is to their advantage.

Hobbes and Locke posit an agreement, not perhaps one in time past, but one whose assumption allows us to make sense of both the obligation to obey the law

[23]Henry David Thoreau, "Civil Disobedience," in *The Development of American Philosophy*. ed. W. G. Muelder and L. Sears (New York: Houghton-Mifflin, 1940), pp. 171, 172.

of the state and the moral permissibility of the state to punish those who do not obey the law.[24] The notion of a contract in Locke is expanded to include an implicit agreement among those who are born into a state but who continue to live in it and to enjoy its benefits.

In contemporary philosophy the device of a contract has been modified and used in a more general way by John Rawls. In this passage he describes what he calls the *original position:*

> The original position of equality corresponds to the state of nature in the traditional theory of the social contract....It is understood as a purely hypothetical situation characterized as to lead to a certain conception of justice. Among the essential features of this situation is that no one knows his place in society, his class position or social status, nor does any one know his fortune in the distribution of natural assets and abilities, his intelligence, strength and the like. I shall even assume that the parties do not know their conceptions of the good or their special psychological propensities.[25]

Rawls adds something that makes his view very close to that of Hobbes. He excludes interest in the welfare of others, and has, in effect, people pursuing only their own interests. In the following passage he disavows a kind of egoism that is limited in interests, but he does not disavow egoism. Indeed, he needs an assumption that each person in the original position looks after his or her own interest and not anyone else's.

> ...think of the parties in the original position as rational and mutually disinterested. This does not mean that the parties are egoists, that is, individuals with only certain kinds of interests, say in wealth, prestige, and domination. But they are conceived as not taking an interest in one another's interests.[26]

The picture, then, in this modern form of contractarianism is that each of us will formulate the rules of distributive justice, trying to make sure that our own good will be secured. But behind what Rawls calls the "veil of ignorance", that is, in the original position. So, not knowing what offices I will occupy in society, not knowing if I will rank in the 5th or 95th percentile in abilities, intelligence, or education, I shall attempt to secure my own self-benefit by formulating some principles of the distribution of the things of value. This will lead us, says Rawls, to posit as an indirect rule of justice that any inequalities of wealth or other things of value will be permitted only if there will be something in it for me, should I not be one of the wealthy. For example, millionaires will be permitted only if the poorest people will be better off with wealthy people than they would be without wealthy people in society. We are not so much interested in Rawls' proposed indirect rules of distributive justice as we are in the device for generating moral rules.

---

[24]See, for example, Thomas Hobbes, *Leviathan* (Indianapolis: The Bobbs-Merrill Company, 1958), pp. 110–119. The material is in Part I, chapter 14. See also, John Locke.

[25]John Rawls, *A Theory of Justice* (Cambridge, Mass.: Harvard University Press, 1971), p. 12.

[26]Ibid., p. 13.

Many people today, though not Rawls himself, use the device of the original position to generate direct moral rules, the DMRs. "Would I, in the original position, adopt the DMR 'If any action is one of lying then it is wrong?' " In this way we have a device for generating DMRs that is an alternative to the principle of utility taken as an indirect moral rule (IMR) and Kant's categorical imperative. One can also posit moving behind the veil of ignorance to settle conflicts between two DMRs. As two examples: "In the original position I would say that I would adopt this DMR," or "While behind the veil of ignorance I would say that not hurting your mother's feelings is more important than not lying."

What shall we say about this kind of NET? Again, I remind the reader that Rawls does not try to use the original position in this open-ended way as others have. First, we must note that the move to go behind the veil of ignorance to settle a conflict between DMRs has a problem similar to one a conscience theory has. People who are apparently equally sincere, and who have done what they can to get behind the veil of ignorance, will disagree about how to settle conflicts or even which DMRs to adopt. Since, according to this NET, the original position is the most basic device, we have nothing more basic than the original position to judge whether the results of its application are correct. If there is some test to determine if someone has correctly used the original position, it is likely to be some independent evidence concerning the correctness or acceptability of a DMR or a weighing. But, any device to accomplish those tasks is more basic in the area of ethics than the original-position move. So, that device, whatever it might be, would be the NET, not the original position.

Rawls' device should perhaps be seen as a helpful aid in thinking of which DMRs to generate and not as the basic element of a NET. When taken as a NET it does not fare very well.

SOME CONCLUSIONS

In this chapter the finalists in the quest for best NET have been presented. No theory is free of problems, as indicated in the criticisms. However, the task before us is to find the best NET, not the one totally free of problems. It is only where certain political ideologies have hold, as in Iran or in Albania, that people claim that their view is correct, problem free, and is totally confirmed by any available evidence. In the sciences no one thinks that the currently best supported theory about the world or some part of it is incapable of being false. No one thinks that the accepted theory is perfect as is and cannot be improved. Improvement of theories is a constant process in philosophy, as in all other theoretical endeavors. Recognize the problems with your theory and try to respond to the criticisms.

In this chapter the NETs taken as serious contenders for best theory were presented. The theories most commonly used in contemporary ethical theory are utilitarianism, a prima facie theory, and some kind of contractarian or RIGHTS-based view. There are some Kantians, but not nearly as many as there are representatives of the other views. The utilitarianism of Mill is a view honed sharp by many generations of philosophers trying to perfect it. There are still problems, but it is a good candidate as best theory. The variable-weight or prima facie theory is tempting, though it needs to be supplemented with a theory of how to weigh the competing factors. The methodology of moral negotiation in Appendix C would complete the theory and prevent it from falling back into an intuitionist theory of knowledge. I am not attracted to contemporary contractarianism because of its tie to some form of psychological egoism. I agree with Mill, furthermore, that there is no need to invent a contract in order to account for our obligations to others.[27]

[27]The contractarianism of David Gauthier (as found in *Morals by Agreement* (New York: Oxford University Press, 1986) occupies the attention of many contemporary philosophers.
   If the reader wishes to become more knowledgeable about contractarianism, this is a good book to read.

CHAPTER **4**

Value

Coverage of value theory completes the survey of the areas of normative ethics. In the first three chapters we often mentioned value, especially in the examination of consequentialist theories. Two consequentialist normative ethical theories are egoism and utilitarianism. They each claim that actions are right insofar as they tend to bring about good consequences; ethical egoism limits the good to one's own good, while the utilitarians claim everyone's good must be taken into account. What *is* good or valuable, though, was not specified. Some think that only pleasure is good, while others suppose some one other thing, such as love, is good. In contrast with such views, most people have supposed there are many sources of good. The values posited include pleasure, love, freedom, knowledge, and salvation. In this chapter we shall make clear what value is, and what a theory of value is as part of one's normative ethical theory. After presenting the material on value theory, we shall be in a position to present the last of the finalists for best normative ethical theory concerning the actions of persons. To bring some order into our examination, we need to show how value fits into the framework used in chapters 1–3.

Let us begin with some explanation of key terms so that we will have value terms to work with at least as clear as 'right' and 'RIGHTS'.

TERMS

The key pair of notions will be intrinsic value and intrinsic disvalue. The trick is to make these notions clearer without presupposing a specific theory of value. This can be done by taking the central sense that philosophers have used in this century. That is, something is intrinsically valuable when it is valuable in itself. It is not just valuable for what it leads to. For example, pleasure is useful in getting someone to learn something. We reward the person who solves a problem, thus reinforcing an item of knowledge. Although the pleasure is useful in gaining knowledge, most of us would say that it has value on its own. This is in contrast to, say, the M & M candies that were given as the pleasurable reward for getting the solution. The value of the candy is explained by the pleasure received from eating it or by the knowledge gained from using it as a reward. Because the value of the candy is, as we commonly say, "not in it," this kind of value is called extrinsic value. Extrinsic value is the value something has insofar as it is instrumental in securing something of intrinsic value. As we saw in the pleasure example, though, something can be of intrinsic and extrinsic value at the same time.

Intrinsic disvalue and extrinsic disvalue are related in the same way as intrinsic value and extrinsic value. Something is of intrinsic disvalue when it is disvaluable in itself and not just because of the disvalue it leads to. Pain is the negative value answering to the positive value of pleasure, so it is a clear instance of something disvaluable. If I stub my toe and suffer through a few minutes of excruciating pain, that is a clear instance of something intrinsically disvaluable. The painful toe may then result in my abusing my dog, another intrinsically disvaluable state, as we will suppose. So the pain is both intrinsically disvaluable and extrinsically disvaluable. Extrinsically disvaluable states, though, need not be intrinsically disvaluable. Engaging in unsafe sex, which we can call being in a state of nonprotection against venereal disease, is not something that is intrinsically disvaluable, but it is often extrinsically disvaluable. If one should contract syphilis or become infected with HIV, that is certain to lead to states that are intrinsically disvaluable.

While there are continuing disputes about exactly which things are intrinsically valuable, almost everyone would agree that pleasure is one of those. Consider the euphoria of a drunken state as a clear instance of such an experience. In contrast, the hangover I have the next day with all its attendant misery is a clear instance of an intrinsically disvaluable state. The pleasure is good in itself, and the pain and misery are bad or disvaluable in themselves. Suppose, though, that as a result of the hangover I vow never to drink too much again, thus leading to a condition of greater health (an intrinsic value). In this instance the intrinsically disvaluable state (the discomfort of the hangover) was *extrinsically* valuable since it led to some intrinsic value. The only combination that is not possible is for some one thing[1] to be both intrinsically valuable

---

[1]The term 'thing' in English is a useful one because it allows one to talk about different categories using just one term. The kinds of "things" that are said to be intrinsically valuable are experiences, relations, people, institutions and many others. Very few objects such as trees or buildings have ever been thought to be intrinsically valuable or disvaluable. So, do not think of the classes of proposed intrinsically valuable or disvaluable candidates as primarily or even usually as 'things' in the sense of 'entities'.

and intrinsically disvaluable.[2] To see how these four notions look, here is a brief synopsis of their meaning:

```
Intrinsic value: x is intrinsically valuable when it is good
in itself; its value is not exhausted by the value of what
it leads to.

Intrinsic disvalue: x is intrinsically disvaluable when it
is bad in itself; its disvalue is not exhausted by the
disvalue of what it leads to.

Extrinsic value: x leads to an intrinsically valuable y.

Extrinsic disvalue: x leads to an intrinsically disvaluable
y.
```

Sometimes we might want to say that something has only extrinsic value or only extrinsic disvalue, but these four notions should allow us to say all we want about what is valuable. Although on occasion philosophers talk about what is good/bad or valuable/disvaluable, the above set of terms is commonly used and is neutral with respect to which things *are* intrinsically valuable or intrinsically disvaluable. To determine which things, if any, are intrinsically valuable or disvaluable, we need to inquire into theory of value.

THEORIES OF VALUE

It is one thing to be reasonably clear about what terms mean and another to know how properly to apply them. When we examined ethical egoism, ethical relativism, utilitarianism, prima facie theory, and Kant's view, we examined theories about when properly to apply terms such as 'right' and 'ought'. Such theories are sometimes called *theories of obligation,* to contrast them with *theories of value.* The two kinds of theories make up what we have called normative ethical theory or NET. In order to have a complete NET, one needs to have a theory of obligation and a theory of value. A utilitarian, for example, needs to tell us what things are good; what things replace the term 'good' in the statement "If any action increases overall good, then it is right." It is to this task we now turn.

HEDONISM

A very popular theory of value is that only pleasure is intrinsically valuable. If we put that in our familiar framework, we find there is one rule of value.

---

[2]Ronald Glass, from whose numerous comments on the manuscript I benefited greatly, suggests a counter-example to this contention. He suggests that the feeling of a full stomach against a tight belt is both intrinsically valuable (pleasure from the good meal) and intrinsically disvaluable (discomfort from the belt pressing in one one's stomach). It seems to me that the two states are quite distinct, though they have a common cause, namely, the meal. The meal is then extrinsically valuable and extrinsically disvaluable. At one and the same time and "in" the same place—me—there is both the value and disvalue. But this one place is not one thing that is intrinsically valuable and disvaluable; there are two distinct experiences that have the value characteristics.

```
P1. If anything is an instance of pleasure, then it is
intrinsically valuable.
P2. The experience of eating a hot fudge sundae is an instance
of pleasure.
```
Therefore, C. The experience of eating a hot fudge sundae
is intrinsically valuable.

The first premise is the rule of value that represents the position of hedonism. The hedonist claims that only pleasure is intrinsically valuable, so that all other things that are valuable are only extrinsically valuable. That is, there is only one rule of intrinsic value. The only thing of intrinsic disvalue is pain, and, accordingly, all other disvaluable things are only extrinsically disvaluable.[3] When we examined psychological egoism, we saw that anyone can make such a claim consistent with the moral phenomena. Someone says, "Saving the lives of your buddies by throwing yourself on a grenade that falls into the foxhole is a clear instance of a non-self-benefiting action." The psychological egoist responds, "The person would have felt guilty if he did not sacrifice himself, so he did it to avoid the bad feelings one gets from this guilt." This answer, as we saw in chapter 2, is not plausible, but it is one will meet up with quite often. In a similar way, then, when someone says that kindness, freedom, or love is also intrinsically valuable, the hedonist will claim these are only extrinsically valuable. This is what a hedonist *claims,* but is there any reason to suppose that hedonism is correct other than its claim, shared by all of its competitors, that it can explain the value phenomena?

There is one argument that will be very familiar to the reader from a discussion in chapter 2. The argument is that we are so constructed that we cannot help but seek pleasure and only pleasure. This is just a special case of psychological egoism, something we can see if we state the two together.

```
Psychological egoism: If any action is voluntary, then its
motive is self-benefit.

Psychological hedonism: If any action is voluntary, then
its motive is to secure pleasure (for self).
```

If we call psychological hedonism PH, and the theory of value under discussion value hedonism or VH, the argument now will be seen to be similar to the one claiming a connection between psychological egoism (PE) and ethical egoism (EE).

```
P1. If PE, then EE.        P1. If PH, then VH.
P2. PE.                    P2. PH.
Therefore, C. EE.          Therefore, C. VH.
```

[3]Just as is true of the rules concerning the evaluation of actions, the positive and negative versions of the rules will be counted as one rule. The hedonist has the positive factor, pleasure, and the negative factor, pain, connected with the notions of intrinsic value and intrinsic disvalue, respectively.

In each case the second premise is a proposed psychological theory of motivation, one that is claimed in the first premise to support the normative theory. Psychological hedonism is quite clearly a special case of psychological egoism, derived by replacing the general notion of *self-benefit* with a specific instance of a *value*, namely, pleasure. If the general position is not tenable, then neither is this specific instance. Since it was argued (in chapter 2) that the general position is not tenable, we are justified in rejecting the specific instance that is psychological hedonism.

A more direct criticism would consist of presenting clear instances of proposed intrinsically valuable things sought that are not instances of pleasure. This is easy enough to do. Consider the following: There were many slaves in the U.S. who were reasonably comfortable in their slavery, having benevolent masters. Nevertheless, many of these slaves repeatedly attempted to escape. Some of them succeeded, finally, in finding their way North, or South into the Florida Everglades, where they almost always lived a life of less pleasure but with freedom. These people sought freedom even though it meant less pleasure, so pleasure is not the only thing people seek as intrinsically valuable. Another example is doing daily calisthenics even though it does not increase my pleasure to do them. It makes me healthier and better able to do my work, perhaps, but I do not, as far as I can tell, aim at more pleasure.

We know, as we saw concerning psychological egoism, that the psychological hedonist will claim that one really, perhaps unconsciously, aims at pleasure when I exercise or when the slave attempts to secure freedom. But, one can claim the same for *psychological masochism,* the view that all we really aim at is pain. Whatever kind of explanation the psychological hedonist presents, we can use that form to "show" that psychological masochism is correct also. "Notice that no matter what we do when we receive pleasure, for instance, eat, drink, or engage in sex, there is inevitably some discomfort and at least low-grade pain following. So, what we were really seeking was the pain. We are not aware of this consciously, so we must unconsciously seek for pain." This is not a bad attempt to render the theory consistent with the phenomena, but it does not show that psychological masochism is correct.[4] If it does not, then neither does the same move by the psychological hedonist show that psychological hedonism is correct.[5]

So, the conclusion is that psychological hedonism is not true. But the situation for the value hedonist is worse yet, for the first premise "If PH, then VH", as the following considerations show, also seems not to be true. This is because the content of value claims is different in an important respect from obligation claims. What psychological hedonism would have us accept is that we each pursue only pleasure. However, value hedonism claims that only pleasure is *worth*

---

[4]If you say it does show that psychological masochism (PM) is correct, then inconsistent theories VH and PM are both true. This is not possible. The point is that this clearly unacceptable theory could be made acceptable if we allowed this kind of defense. Since the theory is not acceptable, the defense is not acceptable either.

[5]At the risk of insulting the reader, and because it causes me great pain, I remind you that the above point does not depend upon saying that pleasure and pain are the same. It is a point about how an argument works, not about the content of the argument.

pursuing. A heroin addict may pursue only heroin or the "high" from taking it, but it is not shown thereby to be worth pursuing. Something that is intrinsically valuable is not just pursued: It is worth pursuing, it ought to be pursued for its own sake. Psychological hedonism could show, if it were acceptable, that pleasure is *valued,* but that does not show thereby that it is *valuable.* So, the first premise is suspect, and we have reasons for thinking the second premise is false.

ADDITION TEST

There is an argument against any value theory that claims there is but one thing of intrinsic value that is so important in the history of ethics that we should set it out separately. We will apply it to value hedonism, but it applies to all monist theories, that is, those theories that maintain there is exactly one kind of thing that is intrinsically valuable. The *addition test,* as we shall call it, goes back at least as far as Plato. It begins with a claim by a monist that there is (exactly) one kind of thing that is intrinsically valuable. The next step is to show that we can add an instance of some other kind and thereby increase the overall intrinsic value of the complex created. Since we have more intrinsic value now than we did at first, the conclusion is that the second kind also has intrinsic value. Let us consider an example to make this clearer. A value hedonist claims that pleasure alone is intrinsically valuable. We then say, "Well, imagine now you have a certain amount of pleasure in your life, and things are certainly all right. Suppose though, you compare a life with that amount of pleasure to one to which we then add friendship. Do we not have a life that is more valuable, one with more intrinsic value, than the one with just pleasure alone? If the answer is yes, and few would deny it, then you have admitted an additional intrinsic value, namely, friendship." If friendship is also of intrinsic value, then pleasure is not the only kind of thing that is intrinsically valuable.

To see the structure of the argument, let IV = intrinsic value, p = pleasure, f = friendship, > = greater than.

```
P1. IVp.
P2. IV(p + f) > IVp.
Therefore, C. IVf.
```

One should not take the "greater than" symbol as indicating some strictly quantifiable unit. Pleasure is, we shall assume, only roughly measured. We say such things as "That was more pleasurable than this," but we do not need to suppose that scratching one's head when it itches is 2.3 while drinking water when thirsty is 3.6 on the hedonic scale. We shall suppose, instead, that we can all make rough comparisons of value. The symbol for greater than is intended to represent that and not some more precise function.

The first premise captures the claim of the value hedonist that pleasure is intrinsically valuable. It does not say that it is the only thing of intrinsic value, but it does not say there is anything else of intrinsic value either. It is in the second premise that the additional item is brought in. The value hedonist is asked whether the second premise is true or not. In response the hedonist will typically agree with the premise, at least under one interpretation, namely, that friendship is only extrinsically valuable, not intrinsically valuable. However, as we saw above, that claim can be made for any proposed monist view, even the view that only friendship is intrinsically valuable. Unless the value hedonist allows these other theories the same move it cannot be used by that theorist either. But if the move is allowed for those who claim that only love is intrinsically valuable, for those who choose only knowledge, those who opt for only power or only salvation, and so on, then we are really in trouble. The trouble stems from the fact that now several incompatible theories will be justified in claiming that only their own choice is intrinsically valuable. This cannot be—it cannot be that only love is intrinsically valuable and only pleasure is intrinsically valuable, and only....To avoid this conclusion, we need to disallow the response that leads to that absurd conclusion. When, however, we disallow this response, the value hedonist as well as any other value monist is left without the typical monist response to the addition test, namely, the response that all our added values are actually only extrinsically valuable, not intrinsically valuable, as non-monists claim.

The "pleasure machine" is a variation of the addition test that is widely used and seems to help in understanding the criticism. Physiologists have located what is called the pleasure center in the brain of mammals. A wire can be implanted in this location in the brain of a rat, for example, and it can be taught to stimulate this pleasure center by pressing a bar that closes a circuit. The rat will ignore food and water, even sexual activity when a willing mate is available, and will continue to press the bar. The rats will continue to press the bar until unconscious or dead. However, when the rat is removed from the cage, given a time to recover and then put in the same cage, it will not press the bar. Apparently even rats recognize that value hedonism is an inadequate theory of value.

An electrode can be placed in the pleasure center of humans also. The following is, I believe, purely a thought experiment at this time, but it is technologically possible right now. We can place you in a room so that pressing a bar will stimulate your pleasure center. Suppose we offer to feed you intravenously, to take care of all your financial worries in exchange for your participation in our experiment. You can leave anytime you want, we say, but we both know that once you activate the pleasure centers you will not be able to stop. We will keep you alive and see to all your needs for the rest of your life. We will exercise your muscles and make sure that you will live about the same amount of time you would have had you not chosen to be in our experiment. You will, for the rest of your life, experience nothing but pleasure. The pleasure, furthermore, is pure pleasure. There will be no hangover, no cost the next day in the way of intrinsic disvalue. It is a hedonist's heaven.

If you, as a hedonist, say you would not choose to be hooked up to the pleasure machine, you need to explain this. Those of us who are not hedonists do not have any trouble; we cite other intrinsic values such as knowledge, friendship, love, and more. If all the hedonist can cite is pleasure, though, we can point out that more pleasure will be secured by being attached to the pleasure machine than could be gained in a hundred lifetimes. In addition, there will be no deduction for pain because there will not be any. A hedonist who refuses to be hooked up to the pleasure machine appears thereby to be agreeing to the addition test and its result.[6]

Some hedonists will say that they would refuse because they have been conditioned by society to refuse. This, though, is not a coherent response. They now know, indeed they strongly proclaim, what the one really intrinsically valuable thing is. What difference does it make what others say? They are, in the hedonist's view, mistaken. Once attached to the machine, the other's and their misconception—as the hedonist sees it—will be out of mind. No, the hedonist must either agree that hedonism is not correct or agree that he or she would choose the pleasure machine.[7]

OTHER MONIST THEORIES

Once we claim that there is one kind of intrinsically valuable thing, then on the basis of the addition test we can show that at least two kinds of things have intrinsic value. This argument is applicable to any monist theory in the same manner. The monist who claims that only friendship is intrinsically valuable need only be shown that pleasure plus friendship is more valuable than friendship alone. This would establish that pleasure, in addition to friendship, has intrinsic value. The same argument applies to all monist theories. Some monist choices that have had significant numbers of followers include power (Nietzsche), agapism (love, some Christians), knowledge, virtue, and freedom.

Regardless of the kind of monist theory, though, the addition test applies. Furthermore, the responses of the monist to criticisms will be the same. Once you know how to respond to one monist theory you should be able to make the same response to any monist theory.

NIHILISM

What though, you may ask, about the person who denies there is anything of intrinsic value at all.[8] Since there are no kinds of things that are intrinsically valuable,

---

[6]There is a small technical problem with the example, though it can be fixed. If you are hooked up to the pleasure machine it is difficult to see how you would get needed sleep, and thus you would shortly die. We will fix our machine so that it monitors your vital signs, and when sleep is needed you will be put to sleep and reconnected before you awake from your timed sleep. Your first awareness will be, again, of the pure pleasure.

[7]On occasion a student will say, "I would agree to be hooked up to the pleasure machine." However, on questioning, this has almost always come to the view that consistency with value hedonism requires this response, not that the student actually believes this is true. Consistency is a good thing but not the only good thing. Another value is trying to explain the moral phenomena, but this cannot be done if they are not reported.

[8]Some people who claim there is nothing of intrinsic value do so because they want to deny that intrinsic value is a *thing*. Some philosophers, for example, G. E. Moore in *Principia Ethica* (Cambridge: Cambridge University Press, 1903), do indicate that value terms such as 'good' refer to an entity, good, which is its meaning. No such assumption is made here. To say that some things are intrinsically valuable is to say that the class of intrinsic value is not empty; it is not to make some deep philosophical claim about the nature of what is said to be intrinsically valuable.

such a person claims, there is certainly not more than one. There have been two kinds of philosophers who claim nothing is of intrinsic value. One is concerned to deny there is anything of intrinsic value *under a certain description* of intrinsic value. This philosopher denies there is anything that would be intrinsically valuable *even if nothing else existed*. This description of intrinsic value is given by G. E. Moore, who defines intrinsic value in terms of its continued value, even if it should be the only thing in existence. This is the position denied by philosophers such as John Dewey. Dewey thought that all things were interconnected with other things, that nothing could exist in the kind of isolation that Moore required us to suppose.[9] But, in the sense of 'intrinsic value' used here, the isolation test of intrinsic value is not presupposed or used. So, one might agree with Dewey that there is nothing of intrinsic value in Moore's sense but nevertheless claim that in the sense introduced earlier there are many sources of intrinsic value.

A more serious reservation comes from those who deny the existence of intrinsic value even in the very sense introduced here. Sometimes these philosophers argue that since there is nothing of intrinsic value in Moore's sense, there is nothing of intrinsic value at all. I agree with Dewey and also with the value nihilists who want to deny there is anything of intrinsic value *of this sort*. The argument that starts with the rejection of Moore's view and ends with the rejection of any view of intrinsic value is, of course, not acceptable. It is not acceptable since we have the sense of 'intrinsic value' introduced here, namely, something whose value is not exhausted by the value of what it leads to. We could agree that there is nothing of intrinsic value in Moore's sense, and yet there are many things of intrinsic value after all. So, we will have to look for a more serious argument.

Another part of Moore's view is that intrinsic value refers to something that is an entity, but it is an entity in a special value realm or world. If one had to suppose the existence of a special kind of thing, something that existed in a special realm and could only be known by a special faculty, that would certainly be a reason not to accept such a view of value. Again, though, one need not suppose that value is this special kind of thing that Moore says. Some intrinsic value is a relation such as love or friendship, another is an experience such as pleasure, and yet another is a state such as knowledge. So, one cannot go from a rejection of Moore's entity kind of theory to the rejection of any theory of value. (This topic will be taken up at greater length in the next chapter.)

One thing the nihilist sometimes says is that it is up to the person who claims there is something of intrinsic value to show that there is. How shall we respond to this challenge? The first and primary way is to offer a theory of value that does a reasonably good job in explaining the value phenomena. If one can provide such a theory, as will be done below shortly, that is the most convincing response. Is there such a thing as gravity? Or quarks, the sub-atomic particles? We can

---

[9]Dewey also denied there is a hard and fast distinction between means and ends. The means we use become part of the history of the end as reached. It is just this end, having just those means. So, even supposing that Stalin reached the goal of industrialization, he did so by killing more than eight million peasant farmers.

demonstrate there is by showing that these notions are used in an acceptable theory of physics. However, short of presenting a complete value theory, we can engage in some preliminary reasoning that describes some of the value phenomena that theories of value explain. The phenomena will provide a prima facie reason to suppose there is something of intrinsic value, though what precisely is of intrinsic value will have to be specified by an actual theory of value.

First, let us note that people engage in rational action. When someone closes the door to shut out the cold, this is a rational action because it achieves an end of a certain sort. If I am chilly and open the door, knowing that this will make it yet colder in the room, and my aim is to become warmer, this is irrational. It is irrational because the means used to achieve the end I seek is known not to be effective. In addition to this kind of irrationality, though, is the irrationality of an end sought. Suppose I open the door because it will make me chilly, and yet say that I think that being chilly is something to be avoided, something that is painful, something that is bad. My action of opening the door is irrational because one value phenomenon is that rational action is explained, in part, by the pursuit of what is thought to be valuable. When someone deliberately attempts to secure what we and he suppose is disvaluable, for example, pain, we take that as good evidence of irrationality. If it is sufficiently disvaluable, we take steps to institutionalize the person. Someone who repeatedly pokes holes in his arm with a needle will usually be put in a mental health care facility.

We can be persuaded not to lock someone up if the person can convince us that some plausible good is aimed at. For example, the person poking holes in his arm with a needle might be taking insulin for diabetes. *Now* we understand the situation; the value the person is seeking is an end such as health. But notice, when we offer this kind of explanation we are, in effect, using the distinction between extrinsic and intrinsic value. The end sought—health—is a reasonable candidate as an intrinsic value. The means—injecting insulin for diabetes—is now seen as a reasonably effective way of achieving it; that is, it is extrinsically valuable.

To claim that we organize our thinking in a certain way, of course, is not to establish thereby that we are correct in so organizing our thinking. It does show, though, that there is a system of thought that has achieved a certain success in our everyday lives. The success of something is fairly good evidence of the correctness of what succeeds. If I succeed in opening my office every day with key #BD24, that is very good evidence that it is the correct key to unlock the door. If we organize our lives and our society using a set of concepts, namely, *intrinsic* and *extrinsic value,* we can achieve many of our aims, and that is some evidence that the concepts represent the proper way to describe our individual and collective lives. Someone could always show us that we have made a mistake, but then we would have to be given a replacement for this set of concepts, a set that would do at least as good a job. This is likely to be just a different set of terms that do the same job as the ones chosen here.

Nihilists need to present more evidence, then, before we accept their view. But, this is not to say, yet, that some specific theory of value is correct. We are in the middle of that task, recall, and to it we now return.

PLURALISM

We are looking for a viable theory of value. A theory of value is that part of our NET that will enable us to arrive at justified intrinsic value judgments in the way that our theory of obligation enables us to arrive at justified judgments of right/ought about actions. We have concluded that monistic theories are not correct because the addition test shows that once we allow one kind of thing to be intrinsically valuable, it is difficult to resist the addition of others. We also concluded that there is some reason, from the moral phenomena, to suppose there are at least some things of intrinsic value. This gives us a straightforward way to summarize the argument so far.

```
P1. If there is at least one kind of thing that is
intrinsically valuable, then there are many kinds of things
that are intrinsically valuable.
P2. There is at least one kind of thing that is intrinsically
valuable.
```
```
Therefore, C. There are many kinds of things that are
intrinsically valuable.
```

P1 alludes to the successful use of the addition test, whereas the second premise depends on the argument against nihilism. What does the above argument show? It shows that a pluralistic theory of value, one claiming there are many kinds of things of intrinsic value, is correct. It does not yet tell us *which* things, though the reader is able at this point to use the addition test as well as anyone else. We shall work out some of the details before raising a few more problems.

The term 'pluralism' is often used in the U.S. to mean a kind of tolerance of other's lifestyles, we should note that pluralism is not used here in that sense. It is, instead, the view that there are two or more kinds of things of intrinsic value. It does not imply that we ought to be *tolerant* of someone who thinks, for example, that enslaving people is a permissible way to live. Indeed, it is reasonably clear that democracy does not imply that some ways of treating people are as morally acceptable as any other. To maintain otherwise would be to assert a claim that sounds like ethical relativism, a position that we have discredited.

In what follows we shall use *pleasure, freedom,* and *friendship* as three proposed intrinsically valuable kinds of thing. When we say that all of these are of intrinsic value, we are thereby committed to the claim that value pluralism is true. But to claim that pleasure is of intrinsic value is not to say that some *whole* that involves pleasure, freedom, and friendship in their positive and negative aspects has a surplus of intrinsic value over intrinsic disvalue. Suppose, for example, we offer you a day of what you would find to be of great pleasure, but the price is that you must lure your best friend to our laboratory where we will carry out painful experiments on him or her. If we now consider the pleasure you receive from your day off, just by itself, it has intrinsic value. If we add to it, though, the pain of your friend and the betrayal of your friendship, the whole situation containing all of those elements seems to have a surplus of intrinsic disvalue. If we use the addition apparatus we can, again, have a pseudo-equation.

```
IVp + IDVpn + IDVb = IDV (p,pn,b)
```

What this says is that even though the pleasure (p) is of intrinsic value (IV) the whole situation has intrinsic disvalue (IDV). The betrayal (b) is intrinsically disvaluable, as is the pain (pn). When these are added to the pleasure the net result is still on the negative side of value. The whole is intrinsically disvaluable even though one part is intrinsically valuable.

A prima facie theory of obligation proposes a number of factors, each of which confers a prima facie obligation to do or not to do an action. The actual obligation under a prima facie theory is determined by weighing all the factors in the situation. What we do when we consider the actual value of a situation is very much like that. Each of the kinds that is intrinsically valuable or disvaluable gives us a reason for saying that the whole is intrinsically valuable or disvaluable. Each of the kinds is a value factor. But whether the situation—the whole that contains all the kinds—is intrinsically valuable or disvaluable depends on all the kinds contained in that situation. We then do something like adding up the positive and negative value to arrive at a judgment of actual intrinsic value or disvalue. All of this may seem reasonably clear, though it may take some re-reading to secure the sense; the situation is made less clear by the next rival to the addition test.

ORGANIC UNITIES

There is a rival that is incompatible with the addition test, called the **principle of organic unities**. This principle, as stated by its formulator, G. E. Moore, says that

> ...*the value of...a whole bears no regular proportion to the sum of the values of its parts.* It is certain that a good thing may exist in such a relation to another good thing that the value of the whole thus formed is immensely greater than the sum of the values of the two good things. It is certain that a whole formed of a good thing and an indifferent thing may have immensely greater value than that good thing itself possesses. It is certain that two bad things or a bad thing and an indifferent thing may form a whole much worse than the sum of badness of its parts. And it seems as if indifferent things may also be the sole constituents of a whole which has great value, either positive or negative. Whether the addition of a bad thing to a good whole may increase the positive value of the whole, or the addition of a bad thing to a bad may produce a whole having positive value, may seem more doubtful; but it is, at least, possible, and this possibility must be taken into account in our ethical investigations. However we may decide particular questions, the principle is clear. *The value of a whole must not be assumed to be the same as the sum of the values of its parts.*[10]

The principle of organic unities is inconsistent with the addition test. If the addition test is correct, when two intrinsically valuable things are added, for example, there is always a whole that has more intrinsic value than either of the parts that make up the intrinsically valuable whole. But the principle of organic unities says this is not always so. Sometimes the whole has less intrinsic value than the two intrinsic values added together.

[10]Moore, *Principia Ethica*, pp. 27–28. Emphasis in the original.

The problem is not just that the two principles are inconsistent, though that would be a serious problem. It is, rather, that the approach taken in this work assumes that the addition test is correct. Since the addition test is inconsistent with the principle of organic unities, I must establish that organic unities is not correct. Let us first be as clear as we can about organic unities, and try to show it at its best; then we will look at the argument in favor of the addition test. Unfortunately for our efforts, the only example Moore gives is from art. Certainly a painting may be beautiful, but its left-hand corner may itself not be beautiful. Not every part of something that is beautiful need be beautiful. Indeed, a part of a painting taken by itself may be quite ugly, while the whole painting is beautiful. This example is plausible in art, but it is not clear how to carry it over for intrinsic value. Here, now, is a try at constructing a plausible example of how organic unities is supposed to work.

Suppose you are a young executive who is about to give your first presentation to a large assembly of company officers of a corporation to which you are trying to sell your own company's product. You are very nervous, so you stumble badly in the presentation, making several mistakes. The subsequent humiliation is a good candidate for a state that has intrinsic disvalue. But now let us add some pleasure, a state that we admit has intrinsic value. However, the pleasure belongs to your chief rival in your company whom you notice is watching your presentation. Your rival is gleefully deriving pleasure from your humiliation. If we consider the entire situation consisting of the pleasure and the humiliation, the supporter of organic unities would maintain, we see that this whole is of greater intrinsic disvalue than the humiliation alone. This result, though, is just the opposite of what we would get if the addition test were used. For if we add the intrinsic value of the pleasure to the intrinsic disvalue of the humiliation we should get a lessening of the total disvalue, perhaps even a surplus of intrinsic value over disvalue. Since there is not a decrease in intrinsic disvalue, and, in fact, the intrinsic disvalue is actually increased, the addition test must be mistaken.

To see more clearly what point is made, here is a formula representing the claim. Letting h = humiliation of the executive, and p = pleasure of the rival, we have:

$$IDV(h + p) > IDVh.$$

This is so even though IVp!

The defender of the addition test can, first of all, agree that a whole composed of a mixture of elements—some of them intrinsically valuable, some intrinsically disvaluable, and some of them neither intrinsically valuable or disvaluable—can have a result that is not just the sum of those intrinsic values. This is at least partly accounted for on the grounds that one of the intrinsic values or a value-neutral item can be extrinsically valuable or disvaluable. A hole in one's tooth is neither intrinsically valuable or disvaluable, but it is extrinsically disvaluable for the pain it will lead to. A situation that consists of the pleasure your torturer receives from viewing the hole in your tooth will still usually contain more intrinsic disvalue than value, just considering the non-relational values that are present. This is because your pain is likely to offset, by far, the pleasure your torturer receives. But suppose your torturer is a sadist who derives great pleasure from the suffering of others. In such a situation the pleasure can more than "equal" the pain, resulting in a surplus of intrinsic value over disvalue. Does not that kind of case still show that the addition test is incorrect and the principle of organic unities is correct? Not yet.

We know that relations can have intrinsic value or disvalue. The relation of taking pleasure in the pain of others, sadism, is a disvaluable relation. It is disvaluable as a relation between persons, just as unkindness is an intrinsically disvaluable relation between persons. The unkindness is a relation, not an experience. There are, of course, experiences and not just relations involved in the total situation. For example, if someone says to a musician, "You have a terrible tone," this is likely to cause the person to feel bad. The feeling bad is intrinsically disvaluable but so is the unkindness, the conveying of the judgment to the person, knowing what it means and is likely to cause. The intention, if you wish, is intrinsically disvaluable. Supposing that this is a correct observation, an observation drawn from the value phenomena, we are in a position to respond to the defender of organic unities. The person who takes pleasure from the humiliation of his rival is standing in an intrinsically disvaluable relation to that rival. To take pleasure from the pain of others is meanspirited at best and sadistic at worst. In either instance, or all the places in between, we find an additional disvalue brought into existence. The greater the pleasure of the viewer, the greater the disvalue of this relation. This reaches its culmination in the sadist who revels in the pain of others. Since the intrinsic disvalue of the relationship increases between the two as the pleasure for one increases, the pleasure of the rival or the sadist will not outweigh the intrinsic disvalue of the humiliation (pain) plus the intrinsic disvalue of the relation.

When we consider the character trait of unkindness or of sadism, we have another candidate for an intrinsically disvaluable thing. Taking pleasure in the pain of others is an instance of exhibiting this sort of intrinsically disvaluable character trait. This is an additional intrinsic disvalue that, given the addition test, would show why the pleasure of the unkind person or sadist gives rise to, and is extrinsically disvaluable for, more intrinsic disvalue.

If the above reasoning is correct, then the value phenomenon the defender of the principle of organic unities draws our attention to is explainable without ad hoc devices by the addition test. Of course, as has been asserted many times in this work, any theory can explain any phenomenon. What we need to do is examine how *well* the phenomenon is explained. No one, including philosophers—perhaps especially philosophers—assert something while thinking it is false.[11] Which principle is correct: I have given reasons to think addition is correct and organic unities is not. Addition explains the value phenomenon better than organic unities. You must ask yourself if you agree or not, and also ask why you take the stand you do.

---

[11]We sometimes lie and even sometimes are justified in lying. I am here talking about asserting what you actually think is so.

ULTIMATE VALUE

In the survey at the beginning of this work, there is a pair of passages concerning ultimate value. I shall now try to show that one of those passages is flawed. First, here are the passages to remind you of what the issue is.

A. 1. We value various things such as friendship, pleasure, love, and freedom. 2. All of these, however, will come to an end. 3. Indeed, since each of us will die, each of the things we value will come to an end. 4. If we wish to find some value to our life as a whole, we must find something that is of value forever, something whose value is eternal. 5. (C) **If there is not something of ultimate value, then none of the things we now value are valuable at all.**

The claims in statements 1 and 2 seem unobjectionable, and even 3 is acceptable in one interpretation. The things we value come to an end in one sense but not in another. Suppose you are my friend, but then you die. If we concentrate on the friend part of the friendship, then the friend is gone. However, if we ask about the friendship itself, the story is not quite the same. It is true right now that a friendship lasting ten years possesses intrinsic value. That friendship does not exist now in the sense that the relationship still is active, but the value was not an illusion. It is true now that Napoleon was defeated at Waterloo even though he is not now being defeated at Waterloo. It is true now that our friendship existed between us even though it does not hold between us now.

Is there anything about the notion of intrinsic value that requires that something of intrinsic value continue to exist for it to be true of it that it is intrinsically valuable? Certainly this requirement does not arise from the notion of intrinsic value. It is generally not true of predicates that unless the thing to which the predicate applies exists forever, the predicate does not apply. For example, the walls in my bedroom are blue one year and yellow another year. Even though the walls are not blue now, blue is not thereby shown to be illusory. The color changed, but it continues to be true now that it was blue then. The second passage makes that clear and presents another argument.

B. 1. We think that pleasurable experiences are valuable and painful ones disvaluable. 2. When the pain ends, it is still true of our experience that it was disvaluable. 3. If disvalue does not require something being disvaluable forever, then there is no reason to think that a value such as pleasure or freedom need be valuable forever. 4. Furthermore, value requires contrast; we would not appreciate the value of pleasure if that was all we had 5. But, this requires that pleasurable experiences end. 6. For these two reasons we can see that (C) **nothing need be of ultimate value for some things, whether love or freedom, to be of value.**

In addition to the argument involving the temporal issue (that is, that some values go out of existence), there is the reference to the value phenomena concerning intrinsic disvalue. Even those who are most concerned to assert the eternality of certain values agree that a short life does not diminish the disvalue of what is disvaluable. It is true, of course, that a pain of magnitude n that lasts for 10 minutes is usually worse than one of the same magnitude that lasts for 5 minutes. That is, however, more of what is intrinsically disvaluable, not the difference between what is intrinsically disvaluable and what is not.

An application of the addition test will show more clearly how the argument from intrinsic value is directed against the argument for ultimate value. Suppose someone lives a life that has some significant intrinsic disvalue—for example, they suffer from cancer—to which we add some significant intrinsic value, such as love and friendship. When the cancer victim has the love of a spouse and children plus a number of supporting friends, that is a life better than one in which there is the same suffering from the cancer but without those positive values. Someone who agrees to this has thereby agreed to the intrinsic value of love and friendship. And this agreement shows the person that no reference to ultimate value needs to be made.

One motive for an ultimate value stand comes from the notion of *self-sufficiency*. Some philosophers, most notably Kant and Moore, characterize intrinsic value in terms of what is self-sufficiently valuable. In the discussion of organic unities, it was noted that Moore thinks that a test of intrinsic value is that the candidate would be intrinsically valuable even if nothing else existed. This means that anything that is intrinsically valuable is completely self-sufficient for its value. If we accept that notion, and then notice that all humans and everything we create are not self-sufficient, we become worried about the possible absence of intrinsic value. We think that without intrinsic value our lives would not be worth living. What makes a life meaningful or worth living is a certain kind and amount of intrinsic value. A life without love, friendship, pleasure, or freedom is not worth living.

Once we accept a notion of intrinsic value involving self-sufficiency and yet we note that our life and that of others is not meaningless, we begin to look for what is self-sufficiently valuable. Unless we find that, we think, the value of our lives and that of everyone else is illusory. Some posit a divine being who is of ultimate value, some a goal such as enlightenment, and some a political state such as a classless society. There is a solution to the problem, though, that does not consist of finding something that is self-sufficiently valuable but consists of using a more acceptable notion of intrinsic value. The notion used here has been defended by showing its fruitfulness in explaining the various theories of value as well as in explaining the value phenomena all the theories attempt to explain. Once we use that notion, the temptation to posit something of ultimate value diminishes.

Many who reject the notion of ultimate value believe in a divine being, one who is indeed self-sufficiently valuable. The present argument is not directed against the claim that such a being exists but only against the claim that the existence of that being's value is required to make our relationships, experiences, and the like intrinsically valuable. The classless society may arrive, and we all may achieve enlightenment, but in the meantime there is much of intrinsic value for all of us to appreciate.

HUMAN LIFE

Many people are inclined to think that human life has intrinsic value. Not only do they think that, but they think that human life has the highest intrinsic value there is. Philosophers who think this often are influenced by Kant's view about the dignity and worth of human beings. They think that if we have an obligation to treat each person with respect, allowing that person to make his or her own judgments and act on them, we must be doing so on the basis of the worth of that person's life. So, the person's life is said to have intrinsic value.

A long discussion of the intrinsic value of persons is not possible here, but a different position can be sketched out. I do not think that human life as such has any intrinsic value; I shall now try to show it has only extrinsic value. The workings of the body, the mere fact of consciousness regardless of content, is not worth anything. A position called **vitalism** might claim that life itself is valuable, but most of us think it is what life makes possible that is valuable. Because of life and consciousness, friendship, for example, is possible. When life makes friendship possible, life is *extrinsically* valuable.

Many people who strongly oppose involuntary euthanasia think that only by affirming the intrinsic value of life can we argue against both euthanasia and infanticide. If you kill an innocent person, even if you do it for that person's own good, it is wrong when done without his or her consent. The explanation is that we have a variable-weight obligation not to kill, and even if the person's suffering would end when death comes, the obligation not to override the person's own decision is weightier. It is weightier for a number of reasons, not the least of which is the set of bad consequences that would result from a social policy that would allow such killings. We do not have to posit the value of the life itself. If we can justify this specific judgment and all the others that are clear instances without positing the intrinsic value of life, we are justified in withholding the claim that life has intrinsic value.

The same kind of response is made concerning infanticide. We want to strengthen the character traits that result in protecting and nurturing children and to weaken those that treat children as property or chattel. This kind of reasoning is sufficient for arguing against the moral permissibility of infanticide. We do not have to posit life as having intrinsic value.

I realize this is not a common stand, and instructors may wish to offer additional arguments in opposition to this view. I think that most of the conclusions and positions people want to hold in which they posit the intrinsic value of people we can defend by arguing by means of the notion of obligation as reached by the usual moral factors. If we can do this, as I claim, and there are no further reasons to suppose to the contrary, we are justified in rejecting the claim that life as such has intrinsic value.

VIRTUE

We have yet to examine a virtue theory of right actions. We have so far examined only those theories that propose a number of direct or indirect moral rules. These principle- or rule-oriented theories, taken all together, contrast with a virtue-ethics theory. The reason we have delayed examining a virtue-ethics theory is that a virtue theory makes essential reference to character traits proposed as intrinsically valuable. It would not have been clear what we were talking about if we had covered such a view before we inquired into theory of value. Having done that, we can now examine this last remaining finalist of our theories of obligation and compare it with rule-oriented views.

Virtue theories are usually traced to Aristotle (384–322 B.C.E.), so we should begin with a brief look at what he says.

> Actions, then, are called just and temperate when they are such as the just or the temperate man would do; but it is not the man who does these that is just and temperate, but the man who also does them *as* just and temperate men do them. It is well said, then, that it is by doing just acts that the just man is produced, and by doing temperate acts the temperate man; without doing these no one would have even a prospect of becoming good.
>
> But most people do not do these, but take refuge in theory and think they are being philosophers and will become good in this way, behaving somewhat like patients who listen attentively to their doctors, but do none of the things they are ordered to do. As the latter will not be made well by such a course of treatment, the former will not be made well in soul by such a course of philosophy.[12]

What is a virtue? It is, on Aristotle's view and still today, a *good* (intrinsically valuable) character trait. But what is a character trait? Character traits are relatively stable tendencies or dispositions to act in certain ways, given certain situations. An honest person, one who has the character trait of honesty, has a tendency to return things, to tell the truth, and so on. Of course, some people acquire not this character trait but its opposite, dishonesty. We can, using our value vocabulary, call honesty an intrinsically valuable character trait and dishonesty an intrinsically disvaluable character trait. We are inclined to think that courage is good and cowardice bad, that the former is an intrinsically good character trait and the latter intrinsically disvaluable. We think this, typically, of such pairs as kindness/viciousness, love/hate, or wisdom/foolishness. In sum, then, a virtue is an intrinsically valuable character trait.

Aristotle had a complex theory of the nature of human beings and the world in which they lived in which he embedded his ethical theory.[13] Many parts of his world view have been incorporated into our own view, for example, rational action as the pursuit of what is intrinsically valuable, but many parts have been rejected. This is especially true of Aristotle's views in physical science. Accordingly, we shall present a virtue theory in its contemporary form rather than in its original form in Aristotle.

Aristotle supposed, and we still accept this to a large extent, that virtues are a mean between two extremes. Courage is a mean between what we can call foolhardiness and cowardice; it is not just the absence of fear. Someone who, literally, felt no fear, would not be thought of as courageous at all. The courageous person feels fear, for example, at the thought of entering a burning building, but acts anyway. We do not take the view of a mean applying to everything in nature, but we still tend to think that way.

[12]Aristotle, *Nicomachean Ethics* 1105b, 5–18, translated by W. D. Ross.
[13]If you wish to read a complex and fascinating work that explores the position that social context is important in understanding ethics (as well as everything else), you might read Alasdair MacIntyre, *Whose Justice? Which Rationality?* (Notre Dame: University of Notre Dame Press, 1988).

When Aristotle talks about 'just and temperate' actions, we can take him to be talking about the evaluation of actions. We call actions right or wrong, obligatory or forbidden, but we will suppose this is mostly a verbal difference. The view before us claims that to determine if an action is right, we must make essential reference to the character trait from which it springs. If the character trait is a virtue then the action is right. Bernard Mayo, a contemporary philosopher who follows Aristotle in this view, recognizes that we are still interested in knowing what we ought to do in a given situation.

> Now according to the philosophy of moral character, there is another way of answering the fundamental question "What ought I to do?" Instead of quoting a rule, we quote a quality of character, a virtue; we say "Be brave," or "Be patient," or "Be lenient." We may even say "Be a man": if I am in doubt, say, whether to take a risk, and someone says "Be a man," meaning a morally sound man, in this case a man of sufficient courage...now the question "What ought I to do?" turns into the question "What ought I to be?"—as indeed, it was treated in the first place. ("Be brave.") It is answered, not by quoting a rule or a set of rules, but by describing a quality of character or a type of person. And here the ethics of character gains a practical simplicity which offsets the greater logical simplicity of the ethics of principles. We do not have to give a list of characteristics of virtues, as we might list a set of principles. We can give a unity to our answer.[14]

We have to understand that Aristotle, Mayo, or any virtue-ethics theorist, is not proposing a rule to follow. One might imagine that a rule is constructed that says "If any action is one that would be done by a virtuous man in fulfilling his obligation, then you ought to do that action."[15] This is certainly of the familiar form we have seen at work in other theories, but this is not what the virtue-ethics theorist is proposing. This theorist is suggesting, in contrast, something such as:

```
If a person A is virtuous (has a virtuous character), and
does some action y voluntarily, and chooses to do y for its
own sake, and A does y from a virtuous disposition, then y
is right.
```

This is a true virtue-ethics description of what it is for someone to do what is right, but it is not a rule that can be used by others to find out what is the right thing to do. This sets out a description of what it is for an action to be right but not how we find out that an action is right. Once the appropriate character traits are in place, that is, the virtues, then right action is explainable as noted above. But how does one come to have the virtues?

Virtue theorists will tell you that you must first act the way a virtuous person does. You find a good person, one who is known to be morally wise and who does

---

[14]Bernard Mayo, *Ethics and the Moral Life* (New York: St. Martin's Press, 1958), p. 213.

[15]Virtue ethics theorists such as MacIntyre say that rules are needed to teach the young how properly to act. The young do not yet have the character traits in place from which they will act when mature. We give them, instead, rules to act from until we instill what (we hope) are virtues. Those who are adult moral actors, though, do not have rules from which we act. (See, for example, MacIntyre *Whose Justice? Which Rationality?* pp. 115–119.)

what ought to be done, and then we emulate that person. This is the sort of thing that children do with their parents: Children emulate their parents. But this raises a problem immediately. For, we also know that not all persons are morally wise or virtuous. Indeed, most people are flawed in a variety of ways. If the primary way to find out what is right is to do what a virtuous person does, then we need to know how to find a virtuous person.

We must select a virtuous person to emulate. To select a virtuous person we must recognize the performance of right actions and wrong actions when they occur. But, since right and wrong actions do not come labeled 'right' and 'wrong', we will need to make justified moral judgments in specific instances. But, if we can make specific justified moral judgments, we do not need to find a virtuous person for this purpose. In order to find a virtuous person to emulate so we will be able, finally, to make justified moral judgments, we already have to be able to make justified moral judgments.

However, the point made much earlier by Aristotle should now be resurrected. You will recall, he says that "it is by doing just acts that the just man is produced, and by doing temperate acts the temperate man; without doing these no one would have even a prospect of becoming good." A defender of a virtue-ethics theory might remind us that one does not come to do what is right just by watching others do right actions. What is needed is a period of action in order to build up the character trait. This, so it would be maintained, is accomplished by emulating the virtuous person. You are to do what the virtuous person does. If you aim at being a good driver you do not accomplish this only by reading manuals on how to drive. You need also to do the kind of things that good drivers actually do when they are engaged in driving. Although someone might say that it is conceivable that one could become a good driver without using a good driver as a model or by taking instruction from such a driver, the chances for success are extremely low.

So, given that we become virtuous by acting as the virtuous person acts when exercising a virtue, and practically speaking we learn to do this only when we have a living model before us, our moral education needs a virtuous person. This may be so, the principle-oriented theorist would respond, but the basic way of finding which actions are right cannot be the method of the moral education. It cannot be that, for as adults, we need to have a method of knowing which actions are right in order to find a virtuous person. It is not even the basic method for all children, because we admit that some parents are not virtuous or select a person who is not virtuous as an exemplar for their children.

One last rebuttal on behalf of a virtue ethics is that children do not know what is right or wrong instinctively or by nature—at least not in any consistent way. Children have no choice but to take their parents or some other person of authority as their model to emulate. This is certainly true, though regrettable in some instances. However, since we can talk about bad models, and there are children who, as they mature, reject the model of their childhood, there must be some way other than emulation to arrive at justified moral judgments.

An olive branch held out by the principle-oriented theorists might be a recognition of the importance of character training. Children are trained whether they will it or not. Adults can choose to change their own character or choose someone to help them. This is an important part of our moral lives. However, the principle-oriented theorists maintain, we can act from our own moral judgments and thus acquire character traits. These are moral judgments we must be able to arrive at without having the character traits that we *will* acquire as a result of acting from our judgments. The specific moral judgments are acquired through principle-oriented NETs.

There is no need finally to decide this issue for the reader, for the virtue-ethics theory is the last of our finalists. You should now review the four finalists and decide which of them—utilitarianism, prima facie view, kantianism, or virtue ethics—does the best job in accounting for the moral phenomena.

Once a NET has been chosen, though, the problems are not over. The issue of the status of the moral predicates remains: "What kind of things are moral properties?" We need to ask whether moral claims are true or false in the same sense as claims about the world are true or false. Is David Hume correct when he says that reason is and ought only to be the slave of the passions? When moral judgments lead to action, is this only through an intermediary emotional or affective state, or can a belief be a "spring of action"? These issues and others will be discussed in the next chapter, which concerns questions that arise from the consideration of normative ethics, but is not itself engaged in trying to find the best NET or to apply a NET to a particular problem.

CHAPTER 5

Applied Ethics
and Meta-Ethics

In this last chapter two topics on different levels of generality will be discussed: Applied ethics is much more specific than our earlier ethical theory discussions, while meta-ethics is much more general. This is appropriate, for they bracket normative ethics and show its centrality in a study of ethics. Applied ethics consists of attempts to offer solutions to moral problems or issues. This is sometimes done, as we shall see, by conscious use of a NET, but sometimes it is done by offering arguments that are presented independently of any NET. Such arguments are almost never independent of a NET, though some authors are not as aware of their NET as they might be.

APPLIED ETHICS

The point of covering a few topics in applied ethics is not to settle the issues or even to take a stand on them. The point is to show how the material in this book can be applied to moral problems. The first point to note is the nature of a moral problem or issue. A moral problem occurs when two or more moral factors apply to a situation, and there is difficulty in determining or in agreeing which of them is weightier.[1]

---

[1] I am not assuming that some version of a variable weight or prima facie theory is correct. If one held a version of Mill's theory the issue would be which direct moral rule was the one which would, in this instance, increase overall good. If one chose a direct form of utilitarianism the conflict would be in deciding which course of action is most likely to increase overall good. I choose to use the 'factors' language because it is usable by other theories, though with their own interpretation of how the factors are to be explained.

a single person has a moral problem, that person is unable to decide which of the factors is weightiest. Within a consequentialist view such as utilitarianism, the difficulty is in weighing the values of the likely consequences of two or more alternatives or in deciding which outcome is more likely.

Easy cases do not give us problems. Anyone can choose between the right and the wrong thing to do, or the good and the bad. If we offer you a choice of drinks that are nutritionally the same, but one will be distasteful and the other will be extremely tasty, you will have no trouble choosing. What makes a case difficult is having to decide between competing positive factors or the lesser of negative factors. It is easy to decide to lie to one's mother about how the birthday meal tastes even though two factors—lying and hurting the feelings of others—conflict. The factors that compete in this instance are easy to weigh. So, to state more accurately what a moral problem is, we need to add that the relative weight of the factors is not obvious.

A common explanation of the difficulty in weighing competing factors is lack of knowledge of key issues. For example, Harry Truman was President of the U.S. in 1945 when, as Commander-in-Chief of the Armed Forces, he had to decide whether to drop the atomic bomb on Japan. Many people, almost a half century later, think the decision was easy. This is, though, due primarily to evidence, now available to the public, about what the Japanese government was actually thinking. At the time, the available evidence did not seem nearly as clear. There was strong evidence that pointed to a determined defense of the Japanese home islands. This would have required an invasion by U.S. and other Allied troops and a protracted war before organized resistance ended. Such a series of operations would have resulted in perhaps a million Japanese deaths and perhaps a quarter of a million American and Allied deaths. In addition, there would have been countless wounded and millions of dislocated civilians.

Truman's decision, based on that information, was to drop the bomb. He had to weigh the likelihood of harm of each action and then decide what to do. If he did not drop the bomb and the Japanese did not surrender on the warning of a super weapon, he would have made the wrong choice. If he dropped the bomb but the Japanese would have surrendered without this action, then the deaths in Hiroshima and Nagasaki would have been unnecessary. Truman was, of course, unable to run a controlled experiment. He had, furthermore, conflicting advice from apparently equally competent experts about what to do. In this set of circumstances, as a president recently installed upon the death of Roosevelt, it was no wonder that Truman had difficulty in deciding what he ought to do.

Most of us do not feel morally uncertain; we see no moral dilemma about dropping the atomic bomb or keeping slaves, but that is because we are not ourselves caught in the moral dilemma. In the next few sections I shall try to engage you in some moral issues that are not as clear cut, issues about which there is still significant disagreement. This will enable you to feel the force of moral dilemmas and to see what help you can get from moral philosophy, but also the limitations of this help.

In general, there are some things we must do in order to make progress on moral problems. First, we must clarify the issue. We must be clear about what the moral problem is. This may sound trivial or obvious, but, as we shall see, it is important and often difficult to do. Once the issue is made clear, then it is time, secondly, to offer arguments and, thirdly, to offer rebuttals. The arguments will typically be recognizable as being within a NET. The first issue presented below— whether it is permissible to eat animals or even to raise them at all as is presently done—shows the importance of both of these last two phases. There are two issues that must be distinguished; once distinguished, it turns out that different kinds of arguments are relevant to each. Let us see how this works.

VEGETARIANISM

An increasing number of people in North America and Western Europe are vegetarians. A large number of arguments on both sides of this issue are in the public domain, most of them first presented by lay people, not philosophers or ethicists. Two different issues have to be distinguished at the outset: The permissibility of eating animals and the permissibility of raising and killing animals as is presently done. The latter issue is one on which many who are not vegetarians agree with the vegetarians: That how animals are presently raised and killed is not morally permissible. A large amount of our food is raised on "factory farms." Peter Singer, a utilitarian philosopher interested in applied ethics, has drawn attention to this issue in a forceful manner.

...Under current British practice, a cage for four or five laying hens has a floor area of twenty inches by eighteen inches, scarcely larger then a double page of the *New York Review of Books*. In this space, on a sloping wire floor (sloping so the eggs roll down, wire so the dung drops through) the birds live for a year or eighteen months while artificial lighting and temperature conditions combine with drugs in their food to squeeze the maximum number of eggs out of them. Table birds are also sometimes kept in cages. More often they are reared in sheds, no less crowded. Under these conditions all the bird's natural activities are frustrated, and they develop "vices" such as pecking each other to death. To prevent this, beaks are often cut off, and the sheds kept dark.[2]

The conditions in the U.S. and Canada are no better. Chickens are often the only land-animal food many people will eat because they identify too closely with mammals. But, do we not pay too high a price for our fried chicken or even scrambled eggs if we obtain them at the expense of the suffering of these animals? As a utilitarian, Singer answers yes to this question. He and most utilitarians follow the philosopher Jerrmy Bentham (1748–1832) on the issue of suffering.

The day *may* come when the rest of the animal creation may acquire those rights which never could have been withheld from them but by the hand of tyranny. The French have already discovered that the blackness of the skin is no reason why a human being should be abandoned without redress to the caprice of a tormentor. It may one day come to be recognized that the number of legs, the villosity of the skin, or the termination of the *os sacrum,* are reasons equally insufficient for abandoning a sensitive being to the same

[2]Peter Singer, "Animal Liberation," *The New York Review of Books,* 5 April 1973. Reprinted in *Moral Dilemmas,* ed. Richard Purtill (Belmont CA:Wadsworth Publishing Co., 1985), p. 376.

fate. What else is it that should trace the insuperable line? Is it the faculty of reason, or perhaps the faculty of discourse? But a full-grown horse or dog is beyond comparison a more rational, as well as a more conversable animal, than an infant of a day, or a week, or even a month, old. But suppose they were otherwise, what would it avail? The question is not, Can they *reason?* nor Can they talk? but Can they *suffer?*[3]

As things stand now, in order for you to enjoy eating chicken or beef, some animal must suffer. The steer is not only frequently raised in conditions under which it suffers, but when it is killed, it suffers the terror of knowing others are being killed and that it is soon to die. A consequentialist needs to show that more good is brought about, even though there is the suffering of the animal, or to argue that the suffering of the animal counts for little or nothing. A nonconsequentialist admits the factor of beneficence as relevant, so the suffering is relevant for a prima facie theory also.

Is it plausible to say that the suffering of animals is of no importance? It is difficult to see how. Bentham as well as those in the contemporary animal-liberation movement say this is just speciesism, an unwarranted favoring of one's own species and ignoring other species and their experiences. We insist on anesthesia for our pets because of their suffering, so we recognize that suffering is an evil, something that is intrinsically disvaluable (IDV). Some people used to say that blacks did not really feel pain in the same way that whites did, but this view is not defensible. To maintain such a view about blacks (or whichever group we chose), we would need to throw out most of the science of physiology to hold to this outlook. But this is equally true of animals: Pigs have much the same neuroreceptors as humans; if they did not we would not try experimental anesthesia on them and then apply the results to humans. This is true of all the research we do on animals.

Some responses to the moral problem are not very good, so I will only briefly describe them. You can fill in the details yourself.

Contention: Without food, humans would die.
Response: A well-balanced and pleasant diet is available without any animal products. Millions now are vegetarians.

Contention: God gave the world to humans collectively, and so God gave all its creatures to humans to use as food.
Response: There are many things said in the Old Testament that we do not take literally, for example, the requirement to burn our clothes and bathe if we should sit on a chair sat on by a woman who is menstruating. As was shown in the section of chapter 2 on morality and God, we use a moral test to choose which of the items that purport to be God's message are really from God. Does God ask us to cause suffering? Does God say that only humans shall enjoy life?

---

[3]Jeremy Bentham, *The Principles of Morals and Legislation* (New York: Hafner Press, 1948), chap. XVII, p. 311.

When we are appointed as Stewards of the natural world, are we being given license to destroy it or to cause suffering? Apparently not.

Contention: It is natural for humans to kill and to eat animals.

Response: Any number of behaviors that were formerly said to be natural are now rejected as morally forbidden. These include keeping slaves, beating women and children, letting people starve, and restricting the voting and ownership of property to white Christian males. There may or may not be a natural impulse to kill and eat animals. If there is, there is also undoubtedly a natural impulse to hit those who annoy or anger us. However, we cannot justify hitting someone because the person annoyed us in, say, the classroom. What this would show is that we sometimes have an obligation not to act from certain natural impulses. So, even if it were natural for humans to kill and eat animals after causing them suffering, it would simply identify another class of "natural" actions that we should extinguish.

Contention: The animals are raised for the purpose of being eaten.

Response: If being raised for the purpose of being eaten were all there were to it, then it would be permissible to eat humans raised for that purpose. Furthermore, it is one thing to be eaten and another to suffer before being eaten. In this argument it is the suffering that is found morally unacceptable.[4]

The reader no doubt has the idea by now. In the last response we return to the distinction drawn earlier. Bentham and Singer object to the suffering, not the eating. Is there a way to have the eating without the suffering? Certainly there is a way, though it may not be an economically viable means of providing animal food. We could drug animals and then painlessly kill them while they slept. That would answer the objection of the suffering, but leaving aside the economic problem, would it lay to rest the objections of the staunch vegetarian?

The staunch vegetarian is someone whose bumper sticker tells us that if we love animals we would not eat them. Singer does not focus on our love for animals but rather their autonomy: "...our practice of rearing and killing other animals in order to eat them is a clear instance of ignoring the most important interests of other beings in order to satisfy trivial interests of our own."[5] What is the trivial interest? It is to satisfy

---

[4]Others argue that we have an obligation to let animals choose their own life path, so even the raising of animals by humans is thought not to be morally permitted. This view would condemn the keeping of animals as pets. This more radical position will not be examined here, though you can certainly take it up in class.

[5]Peter Singer, "All Animals are Equal," in his *Applied Ethics* (New York: Oxford University Press, 1986), p. 223.

our palate. The vital interest of the animal is its life, in its choice of both how to live it and to live it at all. So, even if we did not cause animals to suffer, there is still a reason not to eat them—at least according to Singer.

Does autonomy apply to animals in the same way it does to humans? It is not obvious that it does. Try to decide if it does. The notion of autonomy is borrowed from Kant. Does the notion apply to our dog as it does to humans? If not, is there yet some point to Singer's contention about important and trivial interests? If you take up the issue of vegetarianism in your class, you will find you are now in the heart of the discussion. You are in a position to present arguments in a clear fashion concerning an issue made clearer, but not settled, by this discussion.

ABORTION

A good place to begin laying out this issue is with the survey arguments from the first chapter.

A. 1. A fetus is a living human being, not a lizard or wart. 2. Living human beings have a life right. 3. Life rights generate an obligation on the part of others not to kill the being who has it. 4. Abortion consists of killing a human fetus. 5. So, **there is an obligation not to perform abortions.**

B. 1. A "living human being," a being with rights, is a creature with cerebral brain activity. 2. Before the second trimester of development, until approximately the twelfth week, there is no such brain activity. 3. When there is no "live human being," there is no human with a life right. 4. The first-trimester fetus is thus seen not to be a live human being with a life right. 5. Thus, **there is no obligation not to perform abortions within the first trimester or about twelve weeks into the pregnancy.**

In argument B we see the beginning of a dialogue on the issue. One of the first steps in the dispute is to make clear the distinction between the concepts *human being* and *person.* Not all living things that are genetically human are creatures who have a full range (or any) RIGHTS. For example, those who are brain dead but who continue to breath, either with the aid of a ventilator or alone, are not recognized as having a full range of RIGHTS. The patient does not have any awareness, so cannot control property or choose medical treatment. An-encephalic infants, those born with little or no cerebral hemisphere, will never have any awareness. They will not recognize anyone, they will not enjoy pleasures or suffer pain. Those who carry the distinctive human genetic code are genetic human beings. Those who are bearers of RIGHTS are persons.

Given the facts of physiology, some genetic humans are not persons. This means that the abortion issue is not to be settled by establishing the genetic humanity of the fetus. It means, in short, that the argument in A will not carry the day. It does not mean, though, that the argument in B will carry the day.

In order now to proceed, we need to look to other arguments. The issue, though, is clearer. If the argument is to be settled by arguing from personhood, it will have to take a different route. A few suggestions will now be given in the following abbreviated set of arguments:

Contention: A fetus is not now a person, but, in the normal course of events, it will be a person. So, since it will be a person in the future, it must be accorded the RIGHTS of a person now.

Response: The principle used, namely, "If something will in the future be of a certain kind that ought to be treated in a certain way, then that thing ought to be treated in that way now," is too strong. Each of us will, in the future, be a corpse. Given the nature of corpses, we have an obligation to bury or cremate corpses—for reasons of public health as well as esthetic reasons. Furthermore, when someone is a corpse, those of us who stand in a certain relation to that now-dead person have an obligation to hold memorial services, to distribute their belongings and property, and engage in other appropriate activities. However, none of those things should now be done to persons who are not now corpses but who, in the natural course of events, will be corpses.[6]

Contention: Suppose a woman decided to have an abortion so as to spite her husband, or to sell the fetus for fetal research for $95 so she could buy a new pair of shoes that strike her fancy. We recognize that this is not morally permissible. If the fetus did not have some moral standing, some degree of personhood, this would not be true.

Response: There are sources of obligation other than from personhood and other than from the RIGHTS of persons. For example, we have an obligation to insure that children are treated properly, that they are not beaten, abused, or neglected. The kind of character traits that are valuable for proper care of children include concern for living things and an abhorrence of killing. Once we let pass without condemnation the killing of a fetus for trivial reasons, we think there is significant danger that this will carry over into the treatment of persons. This consequentialist reasoning explains opposition to abortions of the sort mentioned above much more directly than some dubious metaphysical claims about the status of the fetus. But, continuing the consequentialist reasoning, if we stop all abortions, we would be creating much more harm than good. Given the non-person standing of a less-than-three-month-old fetus, the present policy concerning abortion (as outlined in Roe vs. Wade) seems best. In Roe vs. Wade the court ruled

[6]I have not reminded the reader for some time that arguments of this type do not consist of comparing the subject matters. The claim is not that corpses are like fetuses in some physical detail. The argument revolves around a principle that is used by those who argue that potential personhood confers actual personhood now. The use of the corpse "scenario" is to show that the *principle* is not acceptable. If the principle is not acceptable and it is what is presupposed in the position, it cannot be used to establish the position.

that abortion in the first trimester was a matter to be decided by the woman and her physician.

Again we shall leave the issue in the middle, having put it on a more interesting footing than the one we began with. Now, at least, we know what to say to those who picket clinics and carry signs that read "Babies killed in here." Given standard English, a baby is the young born to humans.[7] Those are no more babies, those less-than-three-month-old fetuses, than you are a corpse. It can be viewed as an abuse of English in order to move people emotionally, a trick, but not a useful response to a difficult issue. We can begin to understand the competing factors. On the one hand, we want to instill respect for living things, and we want to insure that humanity will have a future. On the other hand, we want to respect the privacy of women and to allow people an opportunity to have children when it would be better for the children and for them. It is not the simple issue portrayed either as killing babies and or as protection of freedom of action to do with one's body as one chooses.

One additional note: The abortion issue, as the debate continues, becomes a social policy problem, not one primarily involving the moral decisions of individual persons. The Supreme Court makes a social policy decision, it does not merely decide about the permissibility of an individual case. While this does not occur in court, the discussion above gradually has shaded into the public policy arena, and that should be noted.[8]

META-ETHICS

There are some issues that arise as a result of an inquiry into normative ethics. Some of these problems concern our knowledge of moral matters, that is, the **epistemology of morality,** and some focus on the nature of what the predicates used in morally are about that is, the **metaphysics of morals.** The two areas are often connected; some argue from claims in epistemology to those in metaphysics,

[7]We all agree that babies ought not to be killed, whether because they are persons or for other reasons need not be established here. If a fetus is a person from the moment of conception, we do not establish that by using the term 'baby' of it. Should we establish personhood, we would still find it useful to use the term 'fetus' to distinguish those human living beings who have yet to be born—who have yet to attain the status of persons. Moral issues are not properly settled by attempting to capture a term or to change the meaning of a crucial term.

[8]As a modest contribution to the public policy debate, I offer the following temporary partial political solution. We can now freeze and, when it is appropriate, later implant embryos that are then brought to term as babies. It would add some cost to abortions, but it would offer an option to be chosen by the woman as an alternative. We would remove and freeze fetus in the very early stages (certainly no more than ten weeks). It would be an option for the woman to claim the frozen embryo within two years. After that time anyone who wished to claim it for her own personal pregnancy could do so. In this way, those who cannot bear to kill a fetus would not have done so, for the fetus is capable of being thawed. It is true that not all frozen embryos can be thawed and successfully implanted, but the rate of success would improve as the procedure became more common.

The proposal is a political compromise, not a solution to the metaphysical problem of personhood.

and some argue in the other direction. I shall begin the section by talking about epistemology, with the discussion leading into metaphysics.

The number of references will be kept to a minimum, for the aim is to introduce students to some issues, not to try to settle them.

EPISTEMOLOGY OF MORALS

Someone might have chosen utilitarianism, or perhaps a prima facie NET, as the one they think best explains the moral phenomena.[9] Having done that, though, and assuming the correct choice has been made, one can still ask about the *objectivity* or lack of it of the judgments that issue from theories. There are at least two levels of judgment: the specific moral judgment (SMJ) and the principle involved in the inference of it. If the rule, DMR or IMR, is one that is irreducibly *subjective,* then so is the SMJ. But what do people have in mind when they talk about objective and subjective?[10]

The first, and I think the primary, question is whether we are entitled to apply the predicate 'is true' to moral judgments in the same sense as it applies to judgments about the physical world. For example, it is true, we say, that the earth is the third planet of the solar system, or the fourth body if we count the sun as the center of the solar system.[11] What we need is an example of a kind of judgment which is not, in this sense, true. A clear instance of such a judgment is the claim that vanilla ice cream is the best. When someone makes this claim, we understand it to be "about the person," and not primarily about the ice cream. We do not say, "You've made a mistake. It is false that vanilla is the best ice cream, chocolate is." The explanation is that we recognize that judgments about taste are not taken as objectively true or false. They are, in some straightforward sense, subjective. Even if we insist such judgments are true, we want to contrast this sense of 'is true' with the objective sense.

The central place of normative ethics should be kept before us in this discussion. When philosophers such as Mill and Kant present a NET, they suppose it is the one true view.[12] Each author not only presents a NET, but he usually also indicates how the correct theory is established as being correct. The most common way to argue for an ethical theory is to attempt to show that it does a better job

[9]Even to state the issue in this way is to take a stand in meta-ethics. In a paper, "The Nature of Ethics," *Journal of Value Inquiry,* 17, no. 3, (1983) pp. 179–183, I argue in favor of the view presented here. In that article, though, I lay out other competing ways in which to conceive of meta-ethics. In this work all I can do is indicate my starting point and direct those who wish to argue about that to a work in which the premises of my view are stated more fully.

[10]The terms used to talk about this issue change from time to time. And sometimes people use the terms to talk about epistemological concerns and sometimes about metaphysical ones. The pairs cognitivism/noncognitivism, descriptivism/prescriptivism, realism/projectivism, for example, all get at the same set of issues. I choose objectivism/subjectivism because the language is commonly used by students.

[11]I shall continue the practice of assuming that a negative and positive pair make up the notion. If it is not true that the earth is the third planet of the solar system, then it is false. It is true, in this same sense of 'is true', that some body is the third planet of the solar system. If we think the geocentric theory is correct, then the sun is the third body from the center of the solar system.

[12]Mackie calls concerns about the matters of normative ethics first-order judgments and what is characterized below as meta-ethics he calls the concerns of a second order. His characterization of the two areas and my characteristics are not precisely the same.

than its rivals in explaining the moral phenomena. This method of arguing for a NET is used by major ethical theorists such as Mill and Kant. J. L. Mackie, who might be called the "father" of the current non-objectivist movement in philosophy, also indicates that he endorses this meta-theory about the nature of ethical theories, though he sets his own view in a nonobjectivist position.

> More congenial to philosophers and more amendable to philosophical methods would be the attempt systematically to describe our own moral consciousness or some part of it such as our 'sense of justice', to find some set of principles which were themselves fairly acceptable to us and with which, along with their practical consequences and applications, our 'intuitive' (but really subjective) detailed moral judgements would be in 'reflective equilibrium'. That is, we might start both with some *prima facie* acceptable general moral principles, and with the mass of *prima facie* acceptable detailed moral judgements, and where they do not fully agree adjust either or both until the most satisfactory coherent compromise is reached.[13]

Mackie thinks that all NETs presuppose some absolutes, a conclusion contrary to the findings in this work.[14] For years I have been giving students a survey containing a choice between such a view and a view involving variable-weight, first-order or direct moral rules. The vast majority rejects the absolutist view and chooses a prima facie account of moral rules. This is not a great deal of empirical evidence, but it is considerably more than Mackie presents. In a similar vein, Mackie tells us that "Disagreement about moral codes seems to reflect people's adherence to and participation in different ways of life."[15] Not being partial to the view that philosophy is not a rational enterprise but instead a description of an entire conceptual framework (a position that is derived from the later work of L. Wittgenstein), this disagreement does not seem to reflect what Mackie says it does at all. The only objection to the kind of explanation given by Mill—namely, that in different locations different means are best used to reach happiness—is rejected because our specific moral judgments would be "objectively true, but only derivatively and contingently—if things had been otherwise, quite different sorts of actions would have been right."[16] Again, Mackie has imposed a requirement that does not belong. Unless objectivism results not only in objectively true specific moral judgments in some direct manner, not through rules that are objectively true, it is not truly objectivism. Where did this requirement come from? The only reason I can think of to include is the supposition that a very strong certainty component be included as part of objectivism. That is, moral judgments are not only objectively true but true without any doubt. I do not think any such requirement is needed, and to include one seems illegitimate.

Mackie is pessimistic about finding any NET that is both not absolutist and lacking a certainty component, but that is not the finding of this work. Even within

---

[13]J. L. Mackie, *Ethics: Inventing Right and Wrong* (New York: Penguin Books, 1977), p. 105.
[14]Ibid., pp. 27–30. In these pages Mackie is continuing the specification of what objectivity requires or is explained as. This is the view of ordinary morality.
[15]Ibid., p. 36.
[16]Ibid., p. 37.

NETs, though, there are subjective theories that purport to capture what is essential to our moral lives. So, let us begin with those theories—since even non-objectivists such as Mackie think this approach is reasonable—and then see if Mackie's pessimism is justified.

In chapter 1 there was a survey topic involving preference, and in chapter 2 a view called a preference NET was examined. In those discussions is contained the first set of moves that will engage us in the continuing dialectical debate. Let us begin with the survey's pair of claims and then look at what was said in those sections:

A. 1. When someone makes a moral judgment, such as "The use of surrogate mothers is wrong," it is usually relevant to ask for reasons. 2. The reasons given include: "The practice would, if accepted, result in the weakening of the family, and it would lead to baby selling." 3. Now, of course, we may disagree with this conclusion and consequently offer our own reasoning to replace it, but we recognize the appropriateness of the procedure. 4. This procedure is the giving, evaluating, accepting, and rejecting of reasons, something that is not just a matter of preference. 5. Thus, **moral judgments are not just a matter of preference.**

B. 1. Two people can agree about all the observable, factual characteristics of vanilla and strawberry ice cream, and yet one prefers vanilla to strawberry and the other chooses strawberry over vanilla. 2. This is true of all matters of preference, of which taste is but one instance. 3. Disagreements about such matters often outlast factual agreement about the matter at hand. 4. A moral example will show how this applies to ethics: Two people will frequently agree that capital punishment does not significantly deter crime, and yet one will hold that we morally ought to have a capital punishment law and the other the opposite view. 5. This kind of phenomenon shows that **morality is primarily a matter of preference.**

In A we are told that one of the activities we engage in when we dispute about moral matters is the giving and evaluating of reasons. This is something that is characteristic of those kinds of judgments about which we do say that they are objective. (This theme is picked up in chapter 2.) If a preference theory is correct, then reasons would not be relevant for moral judgments. But, one thing is clear about moral judgments: The giving and evaluating of reasons are constant features. Since a preference NET cannot account for this phenomenon, that inability weakens the theory. It is an important moral phenomenon, of course, that people do have strong feelings about moral matters. When people firebomb clinics at which abortions are performed, they act on their moral judgment that abortion is murder. Important moral judgments are usually not simply cool rational judgments; they are frequently passionate pleas that lead to extreme action. Any acceptable NET should take this phenomenon into account, but it looks as though it will have to be a theory other than a preference theory.

The point about evidence remains, though we are no longer talking about a preference theory. Some evidence that a specific moral judgment is objectively true (or false) is that we defend and support it in the same way that we do for judgments that are clearly objectively true (or false). Many people have agreed that we support moral judgments in the same way as judgments based on, say, physical evidence, but this is only because we are reasoning then within a commonly accepted NET, such as utilitarianism. When we inquire after the principle itself, then we have left the realm of justification. We have reached the end of the chain of justification within the area of morality and must do something else. I have said that the "something else" is to argue for one's NET in the same way we do as for any hypothesis explaining a set of phenomena. Others have said, though, that at this point the subjective factor enters,[17] through the selection of one's basic device for justifying all the other rules or specific judgments falling under it.

How could we settle this dispute? According to my metaphilosophical position, we must determine whether working on the best explanation model is the best way to settle the dispute: that is, the hypothesis that the correct methodology is that meta-ethical positions are themselves acceptable if they are the best hypotheses concerning a range of phenomena. If one were to accept, though, a certain ideology, such as Marxism, or have a religious commitment to direct communication with a divine being, we would take a different approach. Is the choice concerning which of these more general metaphilosophical approaches itself subjective or objective? Again, once I have made a commitment to the best explanation route, I apply it at every level. Those who choose, say, one of the subjective routes usually at this point claim that they have independent evidence that morality is subjective in ways in which the clear examples of objective judgments are not. And what is that evidence?

The evidence of the difference between morality and, say, astronomy or medicine, argue the defenders of these views, is that there are ultimate moral disagreements, whereas there are no such things in astronomy or medicine. An ultimate moral disagreement is one in which there is a moral dispute about, for example, the moral permissibility of abortion, and the parties to the dispute agree on all the morally relevant but non-moral facts. The person who makes the most and best use of this kind of argument, in my view, is C. L. Stevenson, whose major work, though written in 1944, is still the best of its kind. But is the claim that there are ultimate moral disagreements true?

Before we ask if the claim of ultimate moral disagreement is true, we must ask what kind of claim it is. Those who wish to make this claim see themselves as offering a claim that is *objectively* true, not just subjectively true. If it were only subjectively true, it could not be used as independent evidence in this meta-ethical dispute. But even if taken as objectively true, we need to ask if it is thought to be an empirical claim, such as those made in astronomy and medicine. It would seem that it must be, for otherwise it is a claim to know about a subject matter that is in the world of experience but known independently of experience. None of the subjectivist philosophers cited earlier (for instance, Mackie) hold to that kind of

---

[17]There are many people who have held this position. The most influential include the following: R. M. Hare, *The Language of Morals* London: Oxford University Press, 1964; C. L. Stevenson, *Ethics and Language* (New Haven: Yale University Press, 1944); Mackie, *Ethics: Inventing Right and Wrong*, Wong, *Moral Relativity*. A critical examination of this kind of move, though still with some sympathy for the temptation, is MacIntyre, *Whose Justice? Which Rationality?*

position. If they do not, then we must look to the evidence we find by empirical means, examining actual moral disputes as well as empirical disciplines such as medicine to see if there is the kind of difference claimed.

One of the most intractable moral disagreements concerns the permissibility of abortion. Yet, the defenders of subjectivism claim, all the facts about human development and social conditions are known by the parties to the dispute. They agree, for example, on when an egg is fertilized, what happens in its development, and how far along this development is.[18] Nevertheless, so say the subjectivists, people still disagree on the moral permissibility of abortion. According to subjectivists, this kind of disagreement is not true of topics in astronomy and medicine, our chosen paradigms of objective subjects. As we shall see, though, these claims concerning the subjects of disagreement are themselves not warranted by the empirical evidence.

Let us begin with the abortion debate, since it has been discussed already.[19] In my experience, an experience that includes speaking before many lay groups, the key to the issue is the nature of personhood. If a fetus is, from the moment of conception, a person with all the RIGHTS that clear instances of persons have, then abortion on demand within the first trimester is not permissible.[20] I agree with this conditional statement, but I also agree with the following one. If a fetus is not a person within the first trimester, and the overwhelming majority of pregnancies are not terminated for trivial reasons but for pressing economic and personal reasons, then abortion within the first trimester is permissible. Those of you who have looked at Appendix C, Moral Negotiation, will recognize the methodology proposed there on how to reach at least conditional agreement. There might be some additional item that some would require in the antecedent of one of the statements, but the method of Moral Negotiation allows the addition of such items. What this method shows is not that people reach actual agreement, for that often does not happen. In this instance it will not readily happen because the issue of personhood is difficult to resolve, because it is a difficult issue in metaphysics or in the overlapping area among philosophy, law, and medicine. The dispute is being carried on right now, but the dispute is not directly over the moral issue; the moral issue is dependent on the resolution of the issue of personhood. This is evidence, admittedly in this one instance, that the resolution of moral disputes depends on the resolution of the factual

---

[18]We are limiting the discussion to abortions requiring only the agreement of the pregnant woman and her physician and those within the first trimester. This fits the July 1989 decision in Webster vs. Reproductive Rights. Most people would agree with the reasoning in the Supreme Court decision, Roe vs. Wade, in which that there is a growing "interest" in the welfare of the fetus, which allows the state to regulate or even ban abortions in the third trimester. In the second trimester the state has an interest in regulating abortions to insure the health of the woman. The vast majority of abortions occur within the first trimester.

[19]The discussion here and in Appendix C, "Moral Negotiation," overlap to some extent. The discussion in the appendix is much more detailed.

[20]Even here, though, the position has some flexibility. For example, many pro-life supporters would agree that abortion of a fetus diagnosed as having Tay Sachs Syndrome or to be anencephalic is permissible. I shall ignore this kind of unusual case, though it is important when talking with someone who has an absolutist position about abortion. (What about the pregnant teenager whose fetus is diagnosed as having Tay Sachs who was impregnated as a result of being raped by her father? For the absolutist to allow this abortion is like the plea of an unwed mother that it was only a small baby.)

issues. The evidence of conditional agreement—where the items in the opposing antecedents are themselves empirical—shows this. So, the initial conclusion based on examining an actual, difficult moral dispute is that there are no such things as what the subjectivists call ultimate moral disagreements.

Those who hold to the subjective approach will, almost invariably, say, "But, my good fellow, you have merely shown that people will agree in this conditional way most of the time. You must admit that it is *possible* there will be disagreement even though there is agreement on all the facts." Indeed I do admit this possibility, but the possibility either shows too little or it shows too much. It shows too much in that the same possibility is true of disagreements in medicine and astronomy. It is certainly possible that someone will agree on all the positional sightings of the bodies in the solar system and yet will claim that the earth and not the sun is the center of the solar system. Not only is this a possibility, it actually occurred. For several centuries some people held out for the geocentric (earth-centered) theory as against the heliocentric (sun-centered) theory. Some members of the Flat Earth Society still hold this view. If the possibility of ultimate disagreement shows subjectivity, then astronomy is clearly subjective. There are people today, namely, the Christian Scientists, who agree to all the empirical facts about disease but who claim that germs have only the most indirect role in disease. According to them, the major explanation of disease, a phenomenon on what they think is a lower plane of reality, is failure to get into proper relation with the being of the highest reality, that is, God. Once we get into the proper relation and do not focus on the plane of lesser reality—what the rest of us call the real world—then disease vanishes. So, again, there is not just the possibility but the actuality of disagreement in an area when there is agreement on all the empirical facts in the area. Unless we want now to claim that astronomy and medicine are subjective, the possibility of disagreement cannot be used. Furthermore, even in the "hard" sciences such as physics and chemistry, it is possible for people to disagree on a given claim even though they agree with all the relevant, related facts. This kind of disagreement occurs in the sciences about issues such as how many basic particles there are or how to account for the "missing mass" in the universe.

The argument from possibility would show that every science is subjective. This is too a high price to pay to establish the subjective nature of morality. Someone might nevertheless say that morality and science are both subjective. I would be willing, at this point, to give them their point, but it has lost its sting. We were to be shown a contrast and a difference between morality and science, but now it turns out there is not this difference. If morality is subjective in the same way science is, that is good enough. If morality is subjective in the same way science is, the argument from ultimate disagreement shows too little. It seems to end with the claim that morality is "only" as objective as science. That too is good enough.

The dispute about the objectivity or subjectivity of our moral knowledge has lately started primarily from metaphysical claims and not epistemological ones. So, let us now turn our attention to those claims.

METAPHYSICS OF MORALS

Those who deny the objectivity of morality typically talk about what moral predicates *refer* to. They have in mind, as the paradigm of a philosopher who posits the kind of objective property whose existence they wish to deny, G. E. Moore. For example, Wong tells us:

> Today, few moral philosophers would subscribe to Moore's theory of moral language. Yet he presents the clearest, most straightforward, and detailed theory of how moral terms refer to irreducible moral properties, and *all philosophers who find such a general view appealing must find a way of incorporating these virtues of Moore's theory while avoiding its problems.*
>
> The core of his theory is the notion of intrinsic goodness. That which is intrinsically good possesses a property that is simple in the sense that it cannot be analyzed into component parts, and it cannot be identified with any other simple property.[21]

What is wrong with Moore's view, on Wong's interpretation (which is typical of contemporary philosophers), is that it requires that 'good' function as a predicative adjective while it actually functions as an attributive adjective. When 'good' is used as an attributive adjective, statements are of the form "x is a good y." For example, Martin Luther King, Jr. is a good man" and "Democracy is a good form of government." When 'good' is used as an predicative adjective it has the form "x is good." Plausible examples of this kind of claim would be "Courage is good" and "Friendship is good." This makes it seem plausible that 'good' is a property of courage or friendship in a way in which, say, round is a property of a ball. Though there are variations of Moore's view, says Wong, all such views must fail because " 'Good' does behave like an attributive rather than a predicative adjective."[22]

A short way of describing this objection is to say that objectivity of morality requires that good be a special kind of property in a special realm, a property that would have to be known in a special way. But, there is not such a special property or special realm, nor is there any special way of knowing, as this view requires. I find myself in agreement with Wong's negative claims about Moore, though not for his reasons.

The question to ask, though, is whether objectivity requires the kind of metaphysical view that Moore held. To begin to answer the question, let me first note that Wong and the other subjectivists concentrate on value and not on right and wrong—on theory of value and not on theory of obligation. Theory of value is concerned with non-action items, whereas theory of obligation is concerned with the evaluation of the actions of persons. In both instances the contemporary subjectivist attempts to point out there is no common standard that will prevent ultimate disagreements. This is sometimes put in terms of relativism because of

[21]Wong, *Moral Relativity*, p. 100. Emphasis added.
[22]Ibid., p. 101.

the claim that within a culture there are standards that allow the resolution of disagreement. However, when we have different standards in different cultures, the ultimate disagreement is much clearer.[23] My response to the ultimate-disagreement move and to the disagreement across cultures is the same. As an empirical fact, no such disagreement is found. This can be stated in terms of conditional agreements based on my own experience, or in terms of empirical studies by psychologists such as Lawrence Kohlberg.[24] The setting out of the claims in the conditionals, though, was always done with obligation or right-action claims, not in terms of value. Is value different and so the subjectivity of morality established in the value half of morality even if not in the action-evaluation half? I think not.

Moore thought that the meaning of 'good' was a unique property to which it referred. A correct claim that x is good predicates of x that property. Moore was a utilitarian, so he thought that actions were obligatory when they maximized overall good. Goodness of a specific situation or thing, in contrast, was established by direct perception, intuition if you like. One can propose, though, a non-Moorean account of the meaning of all moral terms.

I agree with the critics of Moore that the meaning of moral terms is not what they refer to, namely a unique, nonnatural property. Meaning is not reference in the moral sphere. Are there other areas concerning which the meaning of the terms is not some object to which the term refers, and yet the judgments that result are objectively true or false? The answer is clearly yes. Consider, for example, the relations *larger than* and *next to*. When I claim that "h" is larger than "a" in the word "that," this claim is something that is objectively true. We do not throw that into doubt by saying there is no *object* that is (the meaning of) *larger than*. The metaphysical status of relations is not very clear, though most agree the relation itself does not exist independently of things that are in the relation. From our unclarity concerning the metaphysical status, though, it does not follow that the judgment that an object is larger than another or next to another is subjective or relative to a standard that exists within a culture. What we have, first, is an account of how to justify judgments of larger than. Following this, we need to find some metaphysical view of the status of the relation. We are not justified in rejecting some mistaken account of the metaphysical status and then concluding that the relation is subjective. If we do not now have an acceptable metaphysical theory of the nature of relations, let us keep looking.

Do we have an acceptable theory about how to justify judgments involving good? That is, do we have an acceptable theory of value? We do if the value pluralism defended in chapter 4 is the best one. Is it the best one? Look at the arguments again if you have doubts. Present better ones if you have them. What is the correct metaphysical account of the status of intrinsic value? I am inclined to agree with the pragmatic view as expressed by C. S. Peirce and John Dewey

[23]See MacIntyre for a very good discussion of this point.
[24]To get a flavor of Kohlberg's view the reader might browse in L. Kohlberg, *The Psychology of Moral Development: Vol. II. Essays on Moral Development.* (New York: Harper & Row, 1984).

that the metaphysical status is the same as that of *solution to problem.*[25] John Dewey likens a solution to a key that fits a lock. The key allows us to open the door, to get where we aim to go. Is the *relation of being a solution* to a problem itself an object, either in this world or in another? Clearly not! Can we say that there are some objectively true or correct solutions to problems? It would seem so. What is the metaphysical status of something being a solution? It is not something that exists in a special realm, nor is it something that we introspect or directly know. A proposed solution is another kind of hypothesis or theory. We are justified in saying something is a correct solution depending on the outcome.

You may not accept the pragmatic account of the metaphysical status of value predicates. You may have another view in mind. Whatever the best account, though, of the metaphysical status of value, we cannot establish its subjective or relativistic status by rejecting the view of G. E. Moore. This is not legitimate because there are other options. One cannot establish relativism by rejecting absolutism, and one cannot establish the metaphysical subjectivism of value by rejecting Moorean objectivism. All are instances of the same mistake. This is not to say that all that needs to be said in the metaphysics of morals has now been said. Much more needs to be said about the metaphysical status of value—I urge people to engage in the philosophical theorizing needed to come up with a good solution to the problem of determining that status.

SPRING OF ACTION

A last reason for subjectivism stems from the concern about what sets people to acting. There are philosophers who, agreeing with David Hume, think that reason is and ought properly to be the slave of the passions. The idea behind this, repeated by contemporary subjectivists, is that action is "triggered by" or is begun only when there is some desire, affective state, or emotion. Desire and aversion are the primary springs of action. It is when one is thirsty that one is "moved to" drink. If there were no such desire or passion, then no action would occur. Passions are contrasted with beliefs, where beliefs are capable of being true or false. The belief that Santa Monica is in California may be supported by evidence or not, it may be true or not, but it, by itself, would never get me to go to Santa Monica. The same is true of all beliefs. Suppose I had the belief that the room was on fire. I might contemplate all manner of things about the fire: It was consuming the curtains, was about to engulf the magazine lying on the rug, the smoke generated by it would soon asphyxiate me, and so on. However, on this view, unless I had a passion such as fear of death or a desire for life I would continue to sit in my chair while the fire consumed me.

Philosophers in the tradition that requires passion for a spring of action note that moral judgments, when accepted, move people to action. Moral judgments

---

[25]The best statements of this kind of view are found in John Dewey, "The Logic of Judgments of Practise," *Journal of Philosophy* 12, no. 19 (September 1915). Reprinted in *Dewey and His Critics,* ed. S. Morgenbesser, (New York: The Journal of Philosophy Inc., 1977). See also John Dewey, *Human Nature and Conduct* (Carbondale: Southern Illinois University Press, 1988). The work was first published in 1922.

are, they note empirically, a spring of action. This requires, then, that part of what it is to be a moral judgment is some passionate element. This element is not going to be the cognitive appraisal but rather the non-cognitive state that moves people to act. This assumption, usually stated as if it were self-evident, is a significant part of what leads people to adopt some form of subjectivism. But is the assumption correct? Again, I think not.

If one thinks of beliefs as mental "balloons," then the subjectivist position makes sense. The seventeenth-century French philosopher and scientist Rene Descartes seemed to think of beliefs as subjective mental items that existed in the mental substance that was the soul. One might think of the balloons that are above comic strip characters that contain the spoken or only thought beliefs of the characters. These are objects we can look at, though we are obviously not moved to act by them. In the same manner, our own thoughts are in "balloons" that we can be aware of. So, I can look at the balloon that says "The room is on fire. Should I remain here I shall surely die" and not be moved to act unless I also have an aversion to death. I hold that this view of belief is not correct.

An alternative view of the nature of belief is the pragmatic view that belief is a disposition to act. A disposition is a characteristic of something, in virtue of which it will act in a certain way or exhibit certain characteristics when something else happens. The fragility of glass is a dispositional property. The dispositional property is shown occurrently when it is struck with a certain force. It is always fragile, but it is not always shattering. It shatters when certain other conditions are present. My belief that walking through the doorway is the method to leave my office is a disposition to act in a certain way when other conditions hold. For example, it is now time to go to class.[26] Given that no other beliefs are activated that conflict with the belief, then I leave my office through the door. There is no reason to posit another mechanism needed to supply the spring of action.

The dividing up of human beings into various "parts" such as reason, emotion, and will is part of an older faculty psychology. There are different human activities or functions, but there is no reason to propose internal parts that correspond to each of the different activities. Is there a separate arithmetic part of the human make-up, or a separate shoe-tying part? There are various parts of the brain involved in different activities, no doubt about it. There are different skills, but there is no need to posit a different kind of thing that moves us to act. We are thinking-feeling-acting beings, as Albert Ellis says. Dividing us up into separate functions is sometimes useful for the purpose of solving problems, as when we say someone has an emotional disorder. However, we should not be mislead by this

---

[26] As is true of any disposition, there is a problem of specifying background conditions. For example, the glass will shatter if struck by a hard instrument of a certain mass at a certain velocity, unless, of course, in the meantime the glass is tempered or made much harder by some other physical event. Beliefs are of variable weight, and there are often competing beliefs. All these details would have to be spelled out, though all that is required here is an alternative. It is not an alternative that is new, for the pragmatic theory has been before the philosophical community for more than a hundred years. Its defenders have been responding to criticisms for all that time also.

functional difference into positing different metaphysical parts or a completely separate psychological mechanism. Does the subjectivist have another reason for claiming that only a desire or passion is a spring of action? Again, let us see it. If not, this kind of reason is justifiably rejected.

Once the temptation to posit a noncognitive spring of action is removed, a major source of the temptation to adopt some form of subjectivism is also removed. As the reader can tell, though, the dispute continues. This is not because there is not some correct answer, but because philosophy is an ongoing activity. This work has attempted to show the student where the ongoing debate has lead thus far. This is something not usually done in introductory physics or chemistry courses but it is essential to give a sense of what philosophy is.

Professions

This work is designed to be used in a variety of ethics courses, including professional and applied ethics courses. So, something ought to be said about the nature of a profession. In addition to presenting a list of clear instances of professions such as law, medicine, teaching, and the military, is there a general way to characterize professions? Though there is no generally agreed upon characterization, the following incorporates most of the features that people think are essential to a profession.

I shall approach the task by listing important senses of 'professional' used in English. As we get toward the end of the list we find the items most important to 'professional' in the full sense of the term.

EXPERTISE

Some people do things with such skill that we say, usually with approval, that they are professionals. The cartoon character Beetle Bailey might be said to be so good at goofing off that his friends, or his antagonist Sgt. Snork, might call him a professional. A hired assassin, a Rubik's cube solver, or a talented amateur photographer can, in this sense, be called a professional. Even though people with a high level of skill are called, in this sense, professionals, they sometimes do not earn a living doing what they do so well.

LIVELIHOOD

For this second sense we add the element of earning a living by performing a task. When people wonder how they will earn a living, they frequently suppose that being in a profession will better secure a steady income. The first two senses are separate, for some who do some things quite well—such as throwing a frisbee—do not earn a living at it. In this economic sense of 'professional' some very few frisbee throwers, efficient cat burglars, and most prostitutes are called professionals.

SPECIAL SKILLS/KNOWLEDGE

As we get closer to what it is to be a professional in the full sense of that term, we add both special knowledge and skills guided by that knowledge. For example, physicians need to have special knowledge about the body that mathematicians or accountants do not. Future physicians study physiology along with zoologists, athletic trainers, and nurses. In addition, future health professionals will typically study pathology, immunology, and microbiology. But the knowledge, by itself, is not enough to make a physician. To be a physician one needs to have more than just the abstract knowledge of how the body works; one needs to know how to apply that knowledge. The professor of physiology knows more than a physician about how the body works, even more about the nature of disease. However, none of us would go to a professor of physiology for treatment of some suspected disease. A physician, for example, must learn how properly to palpate the abdomen. This is not just pressing down on the abdomen in a certain way; it also includes knowing the significance of this feel rather than that. Knowing the significance stems both from the special knowledge and from the special training to acquire the skill to interpret various feelings in light of the special knowledge. The special training requires practice, practice in doing things guided by the special knowledge under the supervision of those who already have the skills and knowledge. When we add this sense of 'professional', we begin to get at what is important to the clear instances of professions.

SELF-REGULATION/CODES

Some activities are regulated by those who participate in them and some are not. Basketball is not regulated by basketball players, not even by all ex-basketball players. Driving a car is not regulated by the group of persons who drive cars. While automobile-license examiners are those who do drive, it is not their driving skill that secures them their job. The standards of driving are set by a legislative body, not by the class of drivers. In contrast with basketball, driving, plumbing, and most other activities that admit people into them, there are those activities in which the standards of practicing the activity and admission into the group of those who are permitted to practice the activity are determined by those who already are practitioners. Physicians and lawyers decide who practices medicine or law. Likewise, a group of these professionals decide who will no longer be allowed to practice the profession. To this end, a code of ethics is written. The code consists of a set of standards, usually said to be minimal standards, that those in the profession are expected to maintain. If these standards are violated, the practitioner is liable to be decertified.

A code of professional ethics contains not just a set of minimal standards but also the ideals of the profession and a set of reasonably specific moral principles. This will be made clearer by looking at a code of ethics such as that of lawyers or physicians. The following is the code of ethics proposed by the American Medical Association. The *shalls* are not predictions of what physicians will do but are moral obligations.

> The medical profession has long subscribed to a body of ethical statements developed primarily for the benefit of the patient. As a member of this profession, a physician must recognize responsibility not only to patients, but also to society, to other health professionals, and to self. The following Principles adopted by the American Medical Association, are not laws, but standards of conduct which define the essentials of honorable behavior for the physician.
>
> I. A physician shall be dedicated to providing competent medical service with compassion and respect for human dignity.
>
> II. A physician shall deal honestly with patients and colleagues, and strive to expose those physicians deficient in character of competence, or who engage in fraud or deception.
>
> III. A physician shall respect the law and also recognize a responsibility to seek changes in those requirements which are contrary to the best interests of the patient.
>
> IV. A physician shall respect the rights of patients, of colleagues, and of other health professionals, and shall safeguard patient confidences within the constraints of the law.
>
> V. A physician shall continue to study, apply and advance scientific knowledge, make relevant information available to patients, colleagues, and the public, obtain consultation, and use the talents of other health professionals when indicated.
>
> VI. A physician shall, in the provision of appropriate patient care, except in emergencies, be free to choose whom to serve, with whom to associate, and the environment in which to provide medical services.
>
> VII. A physician shall recognize a responsibility to participate in activities contributing to an improved community.

GENERAL VALUE

Each of the clear instances of what we call professions attempts to secure a value. This value is widely shared by the society in which the professional practices. For example, health is the general value goal of medicine, justice of law, and peace of the military. One explanation of why these professions are thought to be honorable by most is that they pursue a shared general value goal. The general value goal does not cease to be a value goal because some in the profession do not aim at it or even subvert it. Justice is still a value goal of law and lawyers, even though some small number of lawyers are themselves criminals. There may be some small number of war mongers in the military, but the overwhelming number of professional military people aim at preserving and securing peace. There are many other value goals within professions besides the general value goal. Medicine aims at eliminating suffering, the military at the security of the country, social work at the autonomy of the client, and law at the rule of law. What makes the general value goal worth singling out is that it tends to give the profession its "coloring" and character.

SPECIAL OBLIGATION

Because of their special knowledge and skills, physicians and nurses have an obligation to the sick that lay people do not. This kind of special obligation is also true of firefighters, police, teachers, social workers, military officers, and many others.

Someone who is a professional in the full sense of that term will fall under all of the categories listed above. Some perfectly respectable ways to earn a living, though, will not be professions in this full sense. Plumbers, basketball players, and bus drivers are not self-regulating practitioners. These activities meet some of the conditions listed but not all. In this work and in any anthology on professional or applied ethics, when a profession or a professional is referred to, the key terms will likely be understood as here outlined. Professionals will be those who are professionals in the full sense of the term.

APPENDIX B

Personal

"Morality is a personal matter." This claim is frequently made when people argue for a moral judgment, particularly if it is one they have some difficulty defending. They choose to contrast morality with other areas such as medicine and astronomy and judgments in those areas to show that they do not have to defend their moral stand any more.[1] It is, however, difficult to find any useful straightforward sense in which morality is personal but beliefs in other areas are not personal. That is, we need some sense of 'personal' that would relieve us of the task of justifying moral judgments but not other kinds. Let us examine some of those senses.

OWN JUDGMENT

One clear sense in which something is a personal matter is that an individual draws his or her own conclusion, not taking it from another person. I use my seat belt because I read the statistics about injury rates for those who do not use them compared to those who do. Most states have now passed laws requiring auto seat belt use, so many who would not, on their own, have used seat belts will now do so to escape a penalty. One has made a personal decision, in this sense, if the

---

[1]The person might have the complex discussion about objectivity in mind. If that is so, it is best to look to the section on meta-ethics in chapter 5.

decision is based on one's own assessment of the evidence and not a result either of coercion or accepting what an authority says.

Almost all of what I accept about distances between cities I accept because of what a map shows, not as a result of my own measurement. When I claim that Jupiter is between Mars and Saturn, this is not from my own observation. This is not a personal judgment, in contrast to my use of seat belts based on the judgment that prudence requires one to wear seat belts.

There are many moral matters that we settle not by our own inquiry, but because we accept the inquiry of others. This is true of children until a certain age, at which time we hope that they will begin to make judgments based on their own assessment of the evidence. Moral judgments are frequently more important than distance judgments, so we are inclined to trust others less. Furthermore, we learn that people often base their moral judgments on normative ethical theories we do not agree with. In this sense of personal—the making of judgments based on one's own assessment of the evidence and not on the basis of what some authority has said—moral judgments are more often personal than not. In this sense, though, one is not immune from criticism. Since reasons are always appropriately asked for when a moral judgment is pronounced, others may criticize those reasons. In this sense of 'personal', the criticism of reasons is not justifiably turned aside by saying "This is my personal judgment."

WEIGHING

Most people finally adopt a version of a prima facie theory, the view that there are many variable-weight moral factors. We reach a moral judgment about what our actual obligation is by weighing the various factors that apply in a specific situation. Since there is no set weight among the factors such as truth telling and increasing good, and there is no additional rule that settles the question, each person must make a *personal* judgment about the relative weights of the factors. In this sense, there is no further evidence that can be provided, so some conclude we must know by intuition or directly that increasing good in this set of circumstances outweighs telling the truth.

There are problems with the claim that one intuitively knows something. The problem is that people disagree about what is known. The Nazis claimed to know, in this way, that Aryans were superior to Jews, Slavs, and other supposedly subhuman creatures. It was this alleged knowledge that "justified" them in treating these groups in inhuman ways. We would all reject their claim of being justified, but since this is supposedly the "end of the line" of justification, there are no reasons we can give. Indeed, even in much less dramatic cases such as whether to smoke marijuana or not, there is no way to settle the dispute on this view. This approach holds that all judgments are equally good since there is no way to choose among intuitions. This is a view that seems clearly to be unacceptable, so I would reject the claim that moral judgments are personal in this sense. (You might want again to look at the discussion of a conscience theory in chapter 2.)

SUBJECTIVITY

A major movement in twentieth-century ethics is noncognitivism.[2] A central claim of that view is that moral judgments are not true or false in the sense that judgments of, say, shape or location are. When I say that Alaska is larger than California and Texas combined, this is either true or false depending on what the facts are. However, there is no moral fact of the matter in virtue of which moral judgments are true or false. Furthermore, the defenders of the view maintain, an important part of the very meaning of moral concepts is some affective state of the person making the judgment. Bernard Goetz shot four youths who apparently intended to rob him in the New York subway. If I say "Bernard Goetz ought to have been found guilty of attempted murder," part of the meaning of the moral term 'ought' is a certain attitude toward the decision of the jury and Goetz' action. I may disapprove of both of them, have a negative or "con" attitude toward those actions.

On a noncognitivist account when you make a moral judgment that disagrees with mine, what actually is happening is that I have one attitude and you have another. When you say "I think the Goetz decision was correct; he ought to have been found not guilty of attempted murder," you are expressing your own attitudes. When I have one set of attitudes and you another, this is compatible, and indeed, it is a fact that we each have a certain attitude. What is not true, though, is that one of our judgments must be mistaken if the meaning of the judgment is an expression of our own attitude.

If moral judgments are personal in the sense that they are really "about" our attitudes, and each of us has attitudes that are true of us, independently of any facts of the situation, we have a sense of 'personal' in which moral judgments are beyond most criticism if they are personal. We each report our own attitudes, about which report we are not capable of being mistaken as long as we honestly follow our feelings. So, in this sense of personal, if moral judgments were personal, my report about my own sentiments would end the matter. But is this view correct?

The talk about a fact of the matter is a "red herring." Moral judgments are almost all relational: For example, "John has an obligation pay Nancy back the $5 he borrowed from her and promised to pay back on Monday." Any relational claim is one whose "referent" is not some object in the world, or any other world for that matter. The judgment that in the word 'word' the letter 'r' is to the right of 'o' is true and can be confirmed by those who understand what the relation *to the right of* is. But, the relation is not some additional object that we see in the same way that we see the individual letters. We would not be justified in saying, though, that since there is no object that is the meaning or represents the relation, then relational judgments are personal, an expression of some affective state and thus not true or false in the same way other kinds of judgments are.

Yet the argument above is just a negative one. Is there some positive argument that can be given? Fortunately there is a straightforward argument available. Specific moral judgments are justified when we apply an acceptable NET in an acceptable way.

---

[2]The reader is directed to chapter 5 for the detailed discussion of this position.

Readers of this work have enough practice in this kind of activity to know what this means. When we apply utilitarianism, for example, to the nuclear-freeze issue, as is done in chapter 1 as an illustration, we arrive at a justified moral judgment.

```
P1. If any action increases overall good, then it ought to
be done.
P2. The action of the U.S. to freeze the production and
deployment of nuclear weapons increases overall good.
Therefore, C. The action of the U.S. to freeze the production
and deployment of nuclear weapons ought to be done.
```

There will be disagreements about which of the second premises, the factual claims, is true, with some thinking that a contrary premise is true. However, that disagreement is one that is resolvable without talking about what is "personal" to oneself. We may even disagree about what is good, but that does not make the moral or value judgments noncognitive. An acceptable theory of value is chosen in the same kind of way an acceptable theory of obligation is. When we have justified our choice of a second premise, we have arrived at a justified specific moral judgment, one that is not just an expression of some affective state of a person. If you want to call this objectively true that is all right, and if you do not that is all right also. The main conclusion is that moral judgments are not noncognitive. Given what has been done in the text, I can even assert they are cognitively justified when we correctly apply an acceptable NET with true premises. This is not to specify some sense of 'true' or to supply an "object" to which moral judgments refer. Those who wish to engage in that additional enterprise are encouraged to inquire into that subject.

My conclusion is that there are senses in which moral judgments are personal and others in which, as I have argued, they are not. Some will think I have not yet captured the sense in which they think moral judgments are personal, and that may be. On the other hand, people frequently think they have something clear and correct to say about a topic. Sometimes, though, there is no clear claim to make; it is an unclear assertion that when examined closely reveals nothing over and above the specific, clear issues discussed. This is my tentative conclusion about the notion of personal as it is used about morality.

APPENDIX C

Moral Negotiation

Moral Negotiation is a process I developed in order to allow more fruitful moral discussion between those who morally disagree.[1] The technique is compatible with any of the major normative ethical theories, so adopting the technique does not commit one to some particular NET. I do hold to a NET that has not been presented in the main body of this work, but I shall sketch it out after presenting the technique of moral negotiation.

The method requires the construction of two *moral conditional statements*. In each of the consequents of the conditional statements will be the differing moral judgments held by the disputing parties. At the end of the second phase of moral negotiation, both or all parties to the moral disagreement will agree on the acceptability or truth of *both* conditional statements.[2] In each of the antecedents will be the set of reasons each party has for holding the view stated in the consequent. To understand the claims in this paragraph some of the key notions such as *conditional statement* must be explained.

---

[1] I have written about moral negotiation in a number of places. See, for example, "Moral Dilemmas and their Treatment," in *Moral Education and Kohlberg: Basic Issues in Philosophy, Psychology, Religion and Education*, ed. Brenda Munsey (Birmingham: University of Alabama, 1980), pp. 43 ff. See also, *Strategies of Ethics* (Boston: Houghton-Mifflin, 1978), pp. 158–161.

[2] Many philosophers think of conditional statements only as used in logic. The material conditional, as it is called, is false only when the antecedent is true and the consequent is false. I am not using that sense. The conditional I am using is one used in ordinary discourse, so that in ordinary discourse we can use the term 'true' of many conditionals that most logicians would defer judgment on. Those of you who have studied logic will note that difference in what follows. I shall also say more about the nature of the conditionals in what follows.

A conditional statement is of the form "If...then..." For example, "If today is Monday, then tomorrow is Tuesday," and "If George Bush is a snake, then George Bush is a reptile." Both of these statements are acceptable or true, even though the antecedent, the part that follows 'if', in the second statement is false. Depending on the day you read the first statement, its antecedent will be true or false. Whether the antecedent of that statement is true or false, though, the entire conditional statement is acceptable or true. This enables us to see that the acceptability of conditionals is not a simple function of the truth or falsity of their antecedents or consequents (the part that follows 'then'). We shall frequently work with conditionals whose antecedents are false; these are *contrary-to-fact* conditionals. While there is controversy about how to determine the acceptability of such conditionals, we shall content ourselves with noting that most of us can pick out the acceptable from the nonacceptable ones in most instances. Consider these conditionals, and ask yourself as you read each one if you think it is acceptable or not:

```
1. If Lassie is a cat, then Lassie is a mammal.
2. If Pink Floyd is a person, then Pink Floyd is a mammal.
3. If Lassie is a dog, then Lassie is a reptile.
4. If Centerberg is the capital of Ohio, then Columbus is
not.
5. If Michael Dukakis is President of the U.S., then he is
right handed.
6. If today is Monday, then tomorrow is Wednesday.
```

There are two questions we must keep separate. "Can people generally pick out the acceptable from the unacceptable conditionals?" "What theory of conditionals best accounts for this?" I am concerned only with the first question and not the second. Students and philosophers can see that 3, 5 and 6 are not acceptable, but the rest are. What accounts for this ability is another issue that will not be addressed, but the absence of an explanation of our ability does not show that we do not have it.

It is clear that the conditionals are not being interpreted as material conditionals, or what logicians call material implication. Material conditionals are true when the antecedent is false, but as 6 shows (for non-Mondays) the above conditionals are not always acceptable or true when the antecedent is false. There is philosophical disagreement about whether to call contrary-to-fact conditionals true, and here no analysis is given of why the conditionals are acceptable, so I hesitate to use 'true' of the conditionals. You may, if you wish, and nothing hangs on the use of the term or its non-use either.

To show how the method works, let us look at a past moral issue and then try another one of more contemporary interest. First, let us look at slavery in the U.S. in the eighteenth and early nineteenth centuries. There now follow two conditional statements, each consequent capturing one side of the dispute but aiming at getting all parties to the dispute to agree that both conditionals are correct.

If slavery consists of:

```
1. Taking care of those who are unable to care for themselves,
and
2. Giving a culture to those who had no culture of their
own in Africa, and
3. Supplying a way of life that will bring more happiness
and contentment than blacks could otherwise obtain,
```

then slavery is morally permitted.

If slavery consists of:

```
1'. Holding those who are able to care for themselves against
their will (not-1), and
2'. Imposing a culture on those who had an alternative viable
culture of their own (not-2), and
3'. Making blacks live in a state of unhappiness and
discontent not offset by the various disadvantages of
freedom (not-3),
```

then slavery is not permitted (obligatory not or forbidden).

There are undoubtedly many additional items that you will think of, but that is all right. Any additional item that you think supports one or another of the consequents can be added as an antecedent item. What is claimed is that if we accept all the items in the antecedent, then the consequent will thereby be acceptable. Remember, it does not matter if you think that an item in an antecedent is not true, for accepting the conditional does not require the acceptance of the antecedent items as true. Nor does accepting that the conditional is correct at this stage require thinking that the items are even relevant. To see this point, consider the following conditional: "If Bush is human and left handed, then Bush is a mammal." This is acceptable even though, as we are aware, handedness is irrelevant to whether one is a mammal or not, or whether one is human or not.

What is important about our sample is that it should show how one can accept two conditional statements as true even though one cannot accept both consequents of the conditionals as true. If you find you do not yet agree, ask what additional items you would need to add to an antecedent to make it acceptable, and then add them.

To get the specific moral judgment from the conditional, the antecedent needs to be affirmed. Both antecedents cannot be confirmed because they are incompatible. At most, one of the antecedents can be true. Which one is true? It is the one best supported by the evidence. If you have formed the conditionals properly, the antecedents will contain statements that are, at least in the broad sense, factual claims. Since we are reasonably confident we know how to decide between competing factual claims, we have a method for arriving at justified moral judgments. For this subject matter, we would use the methods of anthropology or one of the other social sciences to show that one of the complex antecedents is true (and the other thus false). In other disputes, other empirical methodologies would be used.

In complex disputes, though, we frequently do not come to an agreement. Below we shall examine the conditionals of the abortion controversy to see more concretely that this is so, and why this is understandable within the context of moral negotiation as a method. The issue will be whether abortion on demand, for whatever reasons, is permitted within the first trimester.[3]

As a preliminary, let us make the issue more specific. First, since the medical dangers to the pregnant woman increase significantly after the first trimester, and since "higher" brain activity does not begin until after the first trimester, we shall limit the discussion to abortion within the first trimester. Secondly, in order to have a greater chance of representing the positions of those who disagree, we shall exclude pregnancies that endanger the life of the woman. Most people agree that abortion under those circumstances is morally permissible. On the other side, abortions chosen because the pregnant woman has a chance to sell the fetus to a laboratory doing experimental work on fetuses would be forbidden. So, we shall exclude such cases also. We shall talk about abortions for a range of reasons, a range that is indicated but not exhaustively specified. It is important to notice that we are talking about adopting a social policy; we are not primarily making moral judgments about specific cases or instances. Frequently we think that a particular instance of actions protected by a policy is morally unjustified and yet the policy is itself justified. For example, the policy of guaranteeing freedom of speech (protected by the First Amendment) is a good one even though gratuitous insults are as much protected as political criticism. When someone says "I think you look ugly tonight," that is typically morally forbidden. We would not, nevertheless, suggest we repeal or even change the First Amendment to exclude such cases. The same is true in what follows. There will no doubt be instances of actions protected under the abortion policy we adopt that almost all of us think are morally forbidden. That is not crucial; the question is whether on the whole the policy does what we aim at, not whether it works in every single instance.

One reason to be included on our list is that the pregnant woman is someone who would suffer some harm if the pregnancy is carried to term. For example, she might be an unmarried high school student who is not likely to finish school if she carries to term and does not want a child. Another reason is that the child or the mother would have a poor quality of life. Some women choose abortion on the grounds that they are not emotionally prepared to be a mother, that bearing a child would have an adverse emotional effect on them, making it likely they would not be very good mothers. A common reason for abortion is lack of financial resources to give adequate care to a child: The woman is working and cannot afford not to work and having a child would make it impossible or extremely difficult to continue work. Other women simply may not want to have children

---

[3]This discussion overlaps with the one in chapter 5, though there are many additional details discussed here not present in that discussion.

at all. These are the kinds of reasons women have for selecting abortion. The discussion below will assume this kind of reason, not the spectacular and usually agreed on cases such as rape or incest, or abortion to prevent the birth of a child of an unwanted sex.

The conditionals are about abortion within the described context. The items in the antecedent are ones actually chosen by students in my course.

If abortion consists of:

```
1. Killing a being who has a full life RIGHT from the moment
of conception, and
2. Carrying out an action that is likely to produce more
harm to the woman in the form of guilt than the harm that
would result from bearing the child, and
3. Adopting this policy will lead to a moral deterioration
of our society's respect for life,
```

then abortion (within the limits described above) is not morally permissible.

If abortion consists of:

```
1'. A woman exercising an "own-body" or privacy RIGHT, and
2'. Aborting a being who is not yet a bearer of full life
RIGHTS (not-1), and
3'. Performing a minor surgical procedure that will take
place in medically high risk "back street" rooms if it is
prevented from occurring legally,
```

then abortion (within the above limits) is morally permissible.

Some of the items might be stated a bit too briefly, so here is a fuller explanation. In 1, the claim is made that the fetus has in common with clear instances of human beings a full life RIGHT. RIGHTS, recall, are true of persons, and they generate obligations on the part of others. If I have a life RIGHT, then you have an obligation not to kill me. This RIGHT could be overridden by other factors such as my shooting people in a crowded restaurant, but still I have it. If a fetus has a full life RIGHT, then, as people argue, since a fetus is innocent of all crimes, we always have an actual obligation not to kill it. The second point on the con side is a proposed empirical claim about the psychological effects of abortion on those who have it. The truth of this claim has to be determined by empirical research, perhaps a sociology or psychology study. Antecedent 3 is also an empirical claim about the consequences of adopting the pro-choice policy. We could confirm this by noting an increase in killings, in policies resulting in more elderly patients not being aggressively treated, and so on.

On the pro side, 1' makes reference to additional RIGHTS, called variously a privacy or body RIGHT. We do generally suppose that each of us has a privacy RIGHT that generates an obligation on the part of others not to interfere with what we do. This is, of course, a prima facie or variable-weight RIGHT, so the obligations are also of variable weight. I have a prima facie obligation not to interfere with what you do, but this is overridden if you do something to harm me or others. So, you can swing your arm as you wish, but not in such a way as to strike me in the nose. Those on the negative or con side do claim that a fetus has a life RIGHT from the moment of conception, so 2′, which is the denial of 1, has to be added. Antecedent 3′ is, like 3, an empirical claim, partly based on what occurred before abortions were performed in hospitals. Again, whether this prediction is true or not is a matter to be decided by those whose expertise covers this kind of issue.

The antecedents are either empirical, as is true of 2 and 3′, or they attribute some moral characteristic of a different type than the one in question. RIGHTS are not predicated of actions; they are true of persons. They function as value predicates do, as we saw in chapter 4. The clearly empirical claims are ones we might have trouble agreeing on, so we might not be able to decide which of them is true. But, this is not an ethical disagreement as such; it is an empirical disagreement. We suppose that we have the means of resolving such disagreements, if not immediately then at some time in the future when our research methods become more sophisticated. The disagreement about RIGHTS and who possesses them is a complicated issue. Some think that RIGHTS are only generated by obligations, but others think they are the basic moral notion in ethics.[4] Some people think that RIGHTS are a special kind of property that is true of persons, and others do not. These disagreements, however, are disagreements about ethical theory and not about the moral issue at hand. It is conceivable that the outcome of this theoretical dispute might effect the moral dispute, and then the items would appear in the antecedents. These topics are not, though, moral issues.

Some argue that a person is a soul, a spiritual substance perhaps, that inhabits the body from the moment of conception. If this is true, then 1 is supported. But, whether this is true or not is not a moral issue. It is not, by the way, a particularly religious issue either. There are some religions that hold such a metaphysical view, but whether the view is correct or not is something to be decided in the appropriate area of philosophy, namely, metaphysics. Arguments relevant to this issue are well known to philosophers. If the views of some particular religion are correct, they are not correct because the religion says so. Most religions now embrace the heliocentric theory, but the theory is not correct because it is embraced by the religion. The religion embraces the heliocentric theory because it is correct. Should a person be a spiritual substance we call a soul, and should souls be present from the moment of birth, then 1 is true. If a person should be a complex biological creature whose RIGHTS are a function of certain characteristics such as ability to feel pain, sentience, and others, then 1 is not true and 2é is. Which of these is correct, however, is not a matter of obligation or value but of the physical or metaphysical facts. Metaphysical facts may be harder to decide than empirical facts, but they are of the same broad category. Whatever they are, they are not moral claims.

So, having the two conditionals and having reached agreement on the acceptability of both does not mean that it will be easy to decide which set of antecedents is correct. It

[4]See the discussion on RIGHTS-based NET's in chapter 3.

would be surprising to discover there was some method that easily settled difficult moral disputes. This method does not enable us, in some mechanical way, to solve our moral problems and disputes. But, if not, why would anyone want to engage in moral negotiation? First, when one uses moral negotiation, the parties start off by cooperating instead of disputing. We talk together to get the items in the antecedents that will lead to our both or all agreeing on the acceptability of both conditionals. This reduces the emotional "heat" of moral discussions, a factor that often contributes significantly to fruitless disagreement. Furthermore, the moral credentials of each party are certified. Each side now sees how the opponent could hold that moral view, since the disagreement will now revolve around factual issues. I agree with you that if your antecedents are true then your moral position is correct, and you think the same of my position. Finally, once conditional agreement, agreement on the two conditionals, is reached, we think we have the methods for resolving the question of which of the two antecedents is true. We have a lot of experience in the successful resolution of factual disputes, so the likelihood of resolving the moral conflict has increased significantly.

The method of moral negotiation, in summary, consists of the following steps:

1. Clarify and make more precise the moral issue.
2. Construct two moral conditionals that all parties to the moral dispute will agree are true or acceptable.[5]
3. Affirm one of the two antecedents to arrive at the specific moral judgment.

In the course of step 2, it will often happen that a value or RIGHTS item is contained in one or more of the antecedents. That is all right, though if there is disagreement about the truth or acceptability of such antecedent items, they will have to be housed in a set of conditionals of their own. If there is agreement, the process can continue to the last step. It should be noted that failure to carry out the last step is not total failure. In my experience, agreeing to disagree—but with the disagreement now being based on a factual dispute—is not a bad place to leave a disagreement. Think, again, of the abortion dispute. If instead of each side thinking the other consists only of morally insensitive louts, or moral cretins, moral tolerance will be made more likely. This will likely result in means other than violence in settling the dispute. That is significant progress.

I promised I would sketch out another NET, one not so far presented in any straightforward way in this work. My own view begins with a variable-weight view. In fact, even to divorce that view from the position of W. D. Ross while continuing to call my view a prima facie view is to set out part of my own position. I need a name for my view, and though it is a name that is not sufficiently descriptive, it is one that has been used already, namely, **act theory.** More specifically, I would call this a conditional act theory, but act theory is good enough. I shall first set out the elements of my view, and then explain them as is needed.

[5]It is not that difficult to get two conditionals that all parties to the dispute agree with, for if someone disagrees, we ask that person what additional items would result in their accepting the conditional claim. Since the person can add whatever he or she wishes, agreement will result.

Someone cannot, of course, add an item that is simply one of the consequents. However, almost any other item is acceptable.

1. Moral factors are variable in weight.
2. Anything can, in some set of circumstances or other, be a moral factor.
3. There is a methodology that can be used to arrive at justified specific moral judgments (Moral negotiation).
4. The basic unit in morality is the moral conditional.
5. Morality is objective.

The first item is covered adequately in the body of this work. The second claim is one that seems benign enough, but it needs more explanation. Most philosophers suppose that there is some finite and specifiable set of factors relevant to arriving at specific moral judgments. In chapter 3 we examined Ross' proposed six or seven such factors. My own view is that moral factors are not some special set of characteristics of actions or situations, but that any factor can be a moral factor depending on the situation. Suppose, for example, that I shout out "I am seven feet tall." This is not true, and I know it, so in this sense I am lying deliberately saying what is false. However, suppose I am trying to give away the position of my fellow spies to the enemy because I have decided to betray my country. Shouting in order to betray is a relevant factor, but lying, in this set of circumstances, is not a moral factor at all. At my trial for treason, no one would use the fact of that lie itself as evidence of a bad character or include it as part of the prosecution case. On the other hand, if you ask me to repay the $10 I borrowed from you, $10 that I have in my pocket and can afford to give you, and I say, "Gosh, I don't have anything with me now, but I'll bring it tomorrow," the factor of lying is a relevant and important moral factor. Although this is just one example, I think it explains the claim that anything can be a moral factor or fail to be such a factor depending on the circumstances.

The third claim of a methodology should be clear enough from the above discussion. Why that methodology is important to my conditional act theory will become clearer in explaining the fourth claim: the moral conditional is the basic unit in the area of morality. What is a basic unit?[6] *A basic unit in a NET is that part of a NET that is used to justify specific moral judgments or rules that are used to justify specific moral judgments but is not itself justified within that NET.* So, the principle of utility is basic within a utilitarian theory of obligation, for all rules or specific moral judgments, depending on the kind of utilitarianism, are justified by that principle, but the principle of utility is not justified by any of those specific judgments or rules. We can understand this notion of "basicness" by means of our experience with plane geometry. We are familiar with the axiom that tells us that when equals are added to equals the results are equal. It is used to justify other claims within plane geometry, but it is not itself justified within plane geometry. It is, to use the term here being explained, basic within the area of plane geometry. We are here, of course, concerned with morality and not geometry. We know what this area is because of our moral experiences and the inquiry in this book.

---

[6]For a more extensive discussion of this topic, see Rosen, "The Nature of Ethics," pp. 179–190. See also *Strategies of Ethics*, pp. 231–238, and the overlapping discussion in chapter 5 above.

Moral negotiation requires us to construct two moral conditionals. This unit contains information about the particular issue being examined and other items as seen from the examples used above. It is this unit that is said to be basic within the area of morality. Ross thinks that the basic unit is a prima facie *principle,* a moral rule that is a general claim. The way the reasoning proceeds is by way of the general pattern of logic used innumerable times in this work.

```
P1. If any action is one of lying, then it is wrong.
P2. Telling your mother you think the birthday meal tastes
great is an instance of lying.
Therefore, C. Telling your mother the birthday meal tastes
great is wrong.
```

Another applicable rule would be "If any action is one of increasing someone's good or benefit, then it is right." This moral rule plus the second premise—that telling your mother the meal tastes great—would increase her benefit and would allow us to reach the conclusion that telling your mother the birthday meal tastes great is right. The way the argument continues, using a standard or Rossian type of prima facie theory, is to state the other relevant applicable prima facie rules and then to weigh the rules. The view I propose is that we construct the relevant conditionals about the *particular situation.* The standard view is that the general statement or moral rule is required for the justification to be correct, but I deny that claim. The former position can be called a **rule theory,** to contrast it with my own act theory. If we reconstruct the birthday meal situation once again, my own view would have the two conditionals:

```
If telling the truth to my mother about how the meal tastes
will hurt her feelings and no additional good will result,
then I ought not to tell her the truth about how the meal
tastes.
```

```
If telling the truth to my mother about how the meal tastes
will not hurt her feelings in some significant way and it
will improve her cooking and she will come to respect me
and my opinions, then I am permitted to tell her the truth
about how the meal tastes.
```

Which of these antecedents is likely to be true? It depends on whose mother we are talking about and what her relationship is with her child. It is not a matter of taste or preference as to which of the antecedents is true. It is not, furthermore, a matter of weighing the rules. Why is that a good thing, not to have to weigh rules?

If we *have* to weigh the two rules "If any action is one of increasing someone's good or benefit, then it is right" and "If any action is one of lying, then it is wrong," we need to have some method or use some criterion. As argued in chapter 3, if we use a criterion, it will itself have to be a rule or it will be some method such as intuition. The positing of intuition, however, is to introduce a method that is apparently open to all. Those who claim to have an intuition about the relative weightiness of rules, however, disagree about the relative weights. If the intuition is the basic unit within ethics, there is nothing else within the area of ethics to settle the conflict. If we say that both specific judgments are correct, this statement has the unacceptable result that contrary judgments are both true at the same time. If we say that one of them is correct, we are left without a method for determining which one.

If we propose a rule, then, as is shown on pp. 55-56 above, the theorist is caught in a vicious infinite regress. The rule could not be a rule of the same type, a direct moral rule (DMR); it would have to be an indirect moral rule (IMR) that is about the prima facie DMR's. This rule cannot be a categorical rule, since that would create a fixed hierarchy. There is no fixed hierarchy in a prima facie theory; that is one of the desirable features. Sometimes truth telling overrides hurting someone's feelings, and sometimes it goes the other way. But, if there are two such prima facie IMRs, there will be an occasion on which the two will conflict. How shall this conflict be resolved? And here the same problem arises again at the indirect level. The conclusion is that the prima facie theory of Ross has no answer to this problem.

The thoughtful reader, at this point, will have noticed that my own NET is radically different from all the principle-oriented views. Any principles we use are not basic units within ethics; they are derivative from the basic units that are the conditionals about the specific situation. Since they are about specific situations, let us call them *singular conditionals*. The introduction of an act theory leaves us with three types of NET's: the rule theories, a virtue-ethics view, and an act theory—the last being the one defended here. But, do we not need principles? There are many rule-theory arguments that try to show that we need to use principles to arrive at specific moral judgments. I have responded to these arguments in other places, but let me present and respond to one now.[7]

The standard arguments in favor of the need for rules in any NET are summarized nicely by R. M. Hare, so we can get a good sense of what they are and how to respond by examining them.

> The first reason [that we need rules] applies to anyone, even a man with complete insight into the future, who decides to choose something because it is of a certain character. The second reason applies to us because we do not in fact have complete knowledge of the future, and because such knowledge as we do have involves principles. To these reasons a third must now be added. Without principles, most kinds of teaching are impossible, for what is taught is in most cases a principle.[8]

Let us begin by examining the use of principles in teaching. Act theorists can admit that what is taught in most cases is a principle, but we may need only summary principles in teaching morality. A moral summary rule is one derived from successful singular conditionals. One way to teach color terms to children who can count to two is to say "Start at the top of the American flag and count the

---

[7]See, for example, *Strategies of Ethics*, chapter 5.
[8]R. M. Hare, *The Language of Morals* (Oxford: Clarendon Press, 1952), p. 60.

first stripe as *one* and the second stripe as *two*. The number one stripe is red, and the number two stripe is white." The rule, while it could be used by someone who can count, is not *required* to justify the specific judgment that this stripe is red. The child may not know that there is another way to arrive at the justified judgment that the stripe is red, but we know there is.[9]

We often use principles to teach. Most of the time, however, we use summary rules; these are not constitutive rules, which are rules that are required for justifying judgments. For example, when we teach American history, we can use the summary rule "In a non-presidential election year, the party out of office gains power." Or, for another type of example, "If an argument has two existential premises and an existential conclusion, then it is invalid." But for some subjects, such as arithmetic, we use constitutive rules to teach students how to justify judgments that fall under those rules. Since this is so, we cannot say that all teaching is done with summary rules (although it may be possible to get along with only such rules), nor can we say that all teaching makes use of constitutive rules. What we must do, then, is determine which kind of rule is used in teaching morality.

The rules used in teaching morality appear to be such rules as "Do not lie," "Lying is wrong," or "Never tell a lie." As we know, there are effective counter-examples to such rules. For example, if one's spouse or date asks "Do I look all right this evening?," one is sometimes permitted to lie if he or she looks terrible. This is sufficient to show that the general statements are challengeable, and that sometimes, when they clash with specific judgments, the specific judgments are accepted over the general statements. Thus we do not always need to use constitutive rules for moral teaching. Furthermore, we have revealed no real need for constitutive rules. When Hare claims that rules are required for teaching, he is right, but summary rules seem to be sufficient.[10]

Hare's first reason for the necessity of principles is that we "choose something because it is of a certain character." He gives as an example: "If I decide not to say something, because it is false, I am acting on a principle, 'Never (or never under certain conditions) say what is false', and I must know that this, which I am wondering whether to say, is false."[11]

When we decide to do something, it would seem that Hare believes our justification (and our reasoning) has the following familiar form:

[9]If the children are color blind or totally blind, there is probably no other way for them to justify color judgments than to use this rule or one like it. But effectiveness of the rule depends upon its having been established by sighted people who did not use the rule.

[10]Someone might say that the use of the counter-example involves a constitutive rule, and it is only because of such a rule that the individual judgments can be used as a counter-example. However, we do not seem to require a rule to justify the individual judgment that is the counter-example. Furthermore, no trouble-free constitutive rule can be found. As soon as we fix up the rule or state a new one, it meets with the same counter-example difficulty. This is a point that will become clearer later.

Finally, the fact that we think we can find counter-examples shows we do not view moral rules as constitutive. We do not look for counter-examples to the rules of games, but we do think it useful to check moral rules for counter-examples.

[11]Hare, *The Language of Morals*, p. 56.

```
P1. If any x is F, then x is M.
P2. This x is F.
Therefore, C3. This x is M.
```

For F, one can put in the appropriate nonmoral expression (such as 'is an instance of saying what is false'); and for M, one can put in the appropriate moral term (such as 'wrong'). We must obviously suppose that premise 1 is a statement of a constitutive rule. If it is a summary rule, then, as we have seen, the effective use of the rule requires that such rules are not basic, that is, such rules are not needed to arrive at justified moral judgments.

Let us first notice that counter-examples are appropriate to instances of premise 1, such as "If any action is an instance of lying, then it is wrong." It is morally permissible to lie in many circumstances; this is something we all know. From this it follows that the principle is not a constitutive principle with respect to such judgments as "John Smith's act of lying is wrong."

The defender of the need for constitutive principles would probably now add conditions to the principle. It would be claimed that the unrestricted principle is subject to counter-examples, but the restricted one (for example, "If any action is an instance of lying to a friend, then it is wrong") is not. However, we are seldom given a restricted principle, nor are we told how to construct one. Furthermore, restrict the principle as you like and as past experience with such principles shows, counter-examples will still be found. If no principles that are free of counter-examples are found, then we have good evidence that we do not need constitutive rules to justify judgments of that sort.[12]

Another temptation at this point is to say that the principles are prima facie constitutive principles. Prima facie principles, though, require some method of settling disputes concerning weighing. However, this is the position that has already been criticized above, where we found that there is apparently no way of accommodating constitutive principles within the context of a prima facie rule theory.

---

[12]One could trivialize the principle completely so that it reads "Any action of lying whose conditions make it wrong to lie is wrong." Now the principle is not subject to counter-examples, but it is no longer required to justify the specific judgment. If we use it in an argument of the form presented, the second premise would be "This is an action of lying such that its conditions make it wrong to lie." This premise is all that is contained in the conclusion, so we do not need the first premise to arrive at the conclusion. Thus, even trivializing the principle in this way does not show that a constitutive rule is required to justify the specific judgment.

We might also restrict the rule in such a way that it uniquely describes the specific act of lying. If this were done, we could provide no counter-examples of the sort that have been presented. Notice, though, that counter-examples could not be provided because we have described the principle so that it only applies to this one case. We did that because we knew that lying was morally permissible in this case; and if we could only restrict the application of the principle to this case, then it would be safe from counter-examples. Now, however, the knowledge that it is morally permissible to lie in this case precedes the knowledge represented by the principle. It precedes it not only temporally, but in every other way. If the knowledge that lying in this case is morally permissible is prior to the knowledge of the principle, then the knowledge of the principle is not required to justify the specific judgment. The principle is not, therefore, with respect to that judgment, a constitutive rule.

Is the act theory an objectivist view? In chapter 2 there was a discussion of a preference theory, in chapter 4 a discussion of value nihilism, and in chapter 5 a discussion of meta-ethical, subjectivist views. There were arguments in all those sections against the claims of subjectivity of moral judgments. A positive argument in favor of objectivity comes from the argument in favor of the conditional act theory. Should this be the correct NET, should it explain the moral phenomena better than any of its competitors, then moral judgments are objective. They are objectively true because the specific moral judgments are reached by affirming a second premise in the usual, empirical reasoning pattern. Those second premises are true or false in the same sense of true and false as any other empirical claim, such as "The earth is a sphere" or "Columbus' population is larger than Cleveland's."

The first premises are the conditional statements, the singular moral conditionals. These are agreed upon by all parties to the dispute. Even though agreement is not the same thing as truth, as I have argued here many times, agreement is some evidence of truth. The more we inquire into a subject, and agreement continues, the more confident we can be of the truth of the claim. This never makes for certainty, not in the sense in which we cannot turn out to be mistaken, but that kind of certainty is not available for anything besides results within axiomatic systems such as logic and mathematics. So, on the basis of a defense of the conditional act theory, in addition to the reasons previously set out, I claim that moral judgments are either objectively correct or incorrect.

Bibliography

General

ARTHUR, JOHN, ed. *Morality and Moral Controversies*. 2nd ed. Englewood Cliffs, NJ: Prentice Hall, 1986.

ASHMORE, ROBERT B. *Building a Moral System*. Englewood Cliffs, NJ: Prentice Hall, 1987.

BAYLES, MICHAEL, AND HENLEY, KENNETH, eds. *Right Conduct: Theories and Applications*. New York: Random House, 1982.

BEAUCHAMP, TOM ET AL. *Philosophical Ethics, An Introduction to Moral Philosophy*. New York: McGraw Hill, 1982.

BOWIE, NORMAN E. *Making Ethical Decisions*. New York: McGraw Hill, 1985.

BRODY, BARUCH. *Ethics and Its Applications*. New York: Harcourt Brace, 1983.

CALLAHAN, JOAN C., ed. *Ethical Issues in Professional Life*. New York: Oxford University Press, 1988.

CAPLAN, ARTHUR, AND ROSEN, BERNARD. *Ethics in the Undergraduate Curriculum*. Briarcliff Manor, NY: Hastings Center, 1980.

FELDMAN, FRED. *Introductory Ethics*. Englewood Cliffs, NJ: Prentice Hall, 1978.

FRANKENA, WILLIAM. *Ethics*. 2nd ed. Englewood Cliffs, NJ: Prentice Hall, 1973.

GRASSIAN, VICTOR. *Moral Reasoning*. Englewood Cliffs, NJ: Prentice Hall, 1981.

OLDENQUIST, ANDREW. *Moral Philosophy*. 2nd ed. Prospect Heights, IL: Waveland Press, 1984.

RACHELS, JAMES. *The Elements of Moral Philosophy*. New York: Random House, 1986.

ROSEN, BERNARD. *Strategies of Ethics*. Boston: Houghton Mifflin, 1978.

SINGER, PETER. *Applied Ethics*. New York: Oxford University Press, 1986.

————. *Practical Ethics*. New York: Cambridge University Press, 1980.
SOMMERS, CHRISTINA HOFF.   *Right and Wrong: Basic Readings in Ethics*. San Diego: Harcourt Brace, 1986.
STERBA, JAMES, ed.   *Morality in Practice*. 2nd ed. Belmont, CA: Wadsworth, 1987.
WELLMAN, CARL.   *Morals and Ethics*. 2nd ed. Englewood Cliffs, NJ: Prentice Hall, 1988.

Animal Rights

MAGEL, CHARLES.   *A Bibliography on Animal Rights*. New York: Centaur Books, 1983.
MILLER, HARLAN B., AND WILLIAMS, WILLIAM H., eds.   *Ethics and Animals*. Clifton, NJ: Humana, 1983.
REGAN, TOM.   *The Case for Animal Rights*. Berkeley: University of California Press, 1983.
————. *The Struggle for Animal Rights*. Clarks Summet, PA: ISAR, Inc., 1987.
SINGER, PETER.   *In Defense of Animals*. New York: Harper & Row, 1986.

Biomedical Ethics

American Institute History Pharmacy,   *The Challenge of Ethics in Pharmacy Practice: A Symposium*. 1985.
ARRAS, JOHN, AND HUNT, ROBERT.   *Ethical Issues in Modern Medicine*. 2nd ed. Mountain View, CA: Mayfield, 1983.
BACH, JULIE, AND BURSELL, SUSAN, eds.   *Biomedical Ethics*. St. Paul, MN: Greenhaven, 1987.
BANDMAN, ELSIE L., AND BANDMAN, BERTRAM, eds.   *Bioethics and Human Rights: A Reader for Health Professionals*. Lanham, MD: University Press of America, 1986.
BEAUCHAMP, TOM L., AND WALTERS, LEROY.   *Contemporary Issues in Bioethics*. 2nd ed. Belmont, CA: Wadsworth, 1982.
BRODY, BARUCH A., AND ENGLEHARDT, TRISTAN.   *Bioethics: Readings and Cases*. Englewood Cliffs, NJ: Prentice Hall, 1987.
COHEN, MARSHALL ET AL., eds.   *Medicine and Moral Philosophy*. Princeton, NJ: Princeton University Press, 1982.
LEVINE, CAROL.   *Taking Sides: Clashing Views on Controversial Bioethical Issues*. Guildford, CT: Dushkin, 1984.
MACKLIN, RUTH.   *Moral Choices: Bioethics in Today's World*. New York: Pantheon, n.d.
————. *Mortal Choices: Bioethics for Today's World*. New York: Pantheon, n.d.
MAPPES, THOMAS A., AND ZEMBATY, JANE S. eds.   *Biomedical Ethics*. 2nd. ed. New York: McGraw Hill, 1986.
MUNSON, RONALD.   *Intervention and Reflection: Basic Issue in Medical Ethics*. 3rd ed. Belmont, CA: Wadsworth, 1987.
ROBISON, WADE L., AND PRITCHARD, MICHAEL S., eds.   *Medical Responsibility: Paternalism, Informed Consent and Euthanasia*. Clifton, NJ: Humana, 1979.
SHELP, EARL E.   *Born to Die? Deciding the Fate of Critically Ill Newborns*. New York: Free Press, 1986.
VEATCH, ROBERT.   *Medical Ethics Reader*. Boston: Jones and Bartlett, 1988.

Social Sciences Research Ethics

BORUCH, ROBERT F., AND CECIL, JOE S. eds.   *Solutions to Ethical and Legal Problems in Sociological Research: Symposium*. San Diego: Academic Press, 1983.
DIENER, EDWARD, AND CRANDALL, RICK.   *Ethics in Social and Behavioral Research*. Chicago: University of Chicago Press, 1979.

Business Ethics

BEAUCHAMP, TOM L., AND BOWIE, NORMAN E. *Ethical Theory and Business*. 2nd ed. Englewood Cliffs, NJ: Prentice Hall, 1988.

BEHRMAN, JACK N. *Essays on Ethics in Business and the Professions*. Englewood Cliffs, NJ: Prentice Hall, 1988.

CAVANAUGH, GERALD F., AND MCGOVERN, ARTHUR F. *Ethical Dilemmas in the Modern Corporation*. Englewood Cliffs, NJ: Prentice Hall, 1988.

DESJARDINS, JOSEPH R., AND MCCALL, JOHN J. *Contemporary Issues in Business Ethics*. Belmont, CA: Wadsworth Publishing Co., 1985.

DONALDSON, THOMAS. *Case Studies in Business Ethics*. Englewood Cliffs, NJ: Prentice Hall, 1984.

HOFFMAN, W. MICHAEL, AND MOORE, JENNIFER M. *Business Ethics: Readings in Corporate Morality*. New York: McGraw, 1983.

MACHAN, TIBOR R. *Commerce and Morality: Alternative Essays in Business Ethics*. Totowa, NJ: Rowman, 1987.

MATTHEWS, J. B., AND GOODPASTER, K. E. *Policies and Persons: A Casebook in Business Ethics*. New York: McGraw, 1985.

POWERS, CHARLES W., AND VOGEL, DAVID. *Ethics in the Education of Business Managers*. Briarcliff Manor, NY: Hastings Center, 1980.

REGAN, TOM. *Just Business: New Introductory Essays in Business Ethics*. New York: Random House, 1984.

VELASQUEZ, MANUEL. *Business Ethics: Concepts and Cases*. 2nd ed. Englewood Cliffs, NJ: Prentice Hall, 1988.

WHITE, LOUIS P., AND KEVIN, WOOTEN. *Professional Ethics and Practice in Organizational Development: A Systematic Analysis of Issues, Alternatives and Approaches*. New York: Praeger, 1985.

Ethics in Education

PAYNE, STEVE L., AND CHARNOV, BRUCE H. eds. *Ethical Dilemmas for Academic Professionals*. Springfield, IL: C.C. Thomas, 1987.

RICH, JOHN M. *Professional Ethics in Education*. Springfield, IL: C.C. Thomas, 1984.

STRIKE, KENNETH A., AND SOLTIS, JONAS. *The Ethics of Teaching*. New York: Teacher's College, 1985.

Engineering Ethics

BAUM, ROBERT J. *Ethics and Engineering Curricula*. Briarcliff Manor, NY: Hastings Center, 1980.

Environmental Ethics

REGAN, TOM, ed. *Earthbound: New Introductory Essays in Environmental Ethics*. New York: Random House, 1984.

SCHERER, DONALD, AND ATTIG, THOMAS. *Ethics and the Environment*. Englewood Cliffs, NJ: Prentice Hall, 1983.

Governmental Ethics

BOWIE, NORMAN E., ed. *Ethical Issues in Government*. Philadelphia: Temple University Press, 1981.

FLEISHMAN, JOEL L., AND PAYNE, BRUCE L.   *Ethical Dilemmas and the Education of Policy-makers*. Braircliff Manor, NY: Hastings Center, 1980.
———— ET AL.   *Public Duties: The Moral Obligations of Government Officials*. Cambridge: Harvard University Press, 1981.
GUTMANN, AMY, AND THOMPSON, DENNIS, eds.   *Ethics and Politics: Cases and Comments*. Chicago: Nelson-Hall, 1984.

Social Ethics

AIKEN, WILLIAM, AND LAFOLLETTE, HUGH, eds.   *World Hunger and Moral Obligation*. Englewood Cliffs, NJ: Prentice Hall, 1977.
BRODSKY, GARRY ET AL., eds.   *Contemporary Readings in Social and Political Ethics*. Buffalo, NY: Prometheus Books, 1984.
MAPPES, THOMAS A., AND ZEMBATY, JANE S. eds.   *Social Ethics*. 3rd ed. New York: McGraw Hill, 1987.

Journalistic Ethics

GOODWIN, H. EUGENE.   *Groping for Ethics in Journalism*. 2nd ed. Ames, IA: Iowa State University Press, 1987.
MERRILL, JOHN C., AND BARNEY, RALPH D. eds.   *Ethics and the Press: Readings in Mass Media Morality*. Humanistic Studies in Communication Arts. Briarcliff Manor, NY: Hastings Center, 1975.
OLEN, JEFFREY.   *Ethics in Journalism*. Englewood Cliffs, NJ: Prentice Hall, 1988.
RAMSEY, DOUG, AND SHAPS, DALE E., eds.   *Journalism Ethics: Why Change?* Los Angeles: Foundation for American Communications, 1987.

Legal Ethics

DAVIS, MICHAEL, AND ELLISTON, FREDERICK A., eds.   *Ethics and the Legal Profession*. Buffalo, NY: Prometheus Books, 1986.
SCHRADER, DAVID E.   *Ethics and the Practice of Law*. Englewood Cliffs, NJ: Prentice Hall, 1988.

Military Ethics

NATIONAL CONFERENCE OF CATHOLIC BISHOPS.   *The Challenge of Peace*. Washington, DC: U.S. Catholic Conference, 1983.
RAMSEY, PAUL.   *The Just War*. Lanham, MD: University Press of America, 1983.
STERBA, JAMES.   *The Ethics of War and Nuclear Deterrence*. Belmont, CA: Wadsworth Publishing Co., 1985.
SCHELL, JONATHAN.   *The Fate of the Earth*. New York: Knopf, 1982.
WAKIN, MALHAM.   *War, Morality and the Military Profession*. 2nd ed. Boulder, CO: Westview, 1979.
WALZER, MICHAEL.   *Just and Unjust Wars*. New York: Basic Books, 1977.
WASSERSTROM, RICHARD.   *War and Morality*. Belmont, CA: Wadsworth Publishing Co., 1970.

Nursing Ethics

APPLEGATE, MINERVA, AND ENTRENKIN, NINA.   *Case Studies for Students: A Companion to Teaching Ethics in Nursing*. New York: National League for Nursing, 1984.

BENJAMIN, MARTIN, AND CURTIS, JOY, eds. *Ethics in Nursing.* 2nd ed. New York: Oxford University Press, 1986.

JAMETON, ANDREW. *Nursing Practice: The Ethical Issues.* Englewood Cliffs, NJ: Prentice Hall, 1984.

PENCE, TERRY. *Ethics in Nursing: An Annotated Bibliography.* 2nd ed. New York: National League for Nursing, 1986.

Mental Health and Social Services

POPE, KENNETH S., AND BOUHOUTSOS, JACQUELINE C. *Sexual Intimacy Between Therapists and Patients.* Sexual Medicine Series: Vol. 5. New York: Praeger, 1986.

REAMER, FREDERICK G. *Ethical Dilemmas in Social Service.* New York: Columbia University Press, 1982.

RHODES, MARGARET L. *Ethical Dilemmas in Social Work Practice.* Boston: Routledge and Kegan Paul, 1986.

WELLS, CAROLYN C., AND MASCH, KATHLEEN M. *Social Work Ethics Day to Day: Guidelines for Professional Practice.* White Plains, NY: Longman, 1988.

Index